An invitation to our readers:
Most of the routes in the GUIDE have been contributed by veteran cyclists who ride the area regularly. But, due to development and construction, the roads are constantly changing. With all our careful editing, we humbly acknowledge that there may still be some mistakes. If you find an error or know of any improvement, please let us know. We will edit before reprinting. We welcome your comments and suggestions.

Address all correspondence to:
Guide To Cycling Kansas City
RECYCLED
c/o Cycle Write Enterprises
P.O. Box 26243
Shawnee Mission, KS 66225

Library of Congress
Cataloging-in-Publication Data
CIP 95-092275
Katz, Steve
125 bicycle tours, on and off road, in and around Kansas City.
ISBN 0-9632730-3-5

Published by
Cycle Write Enterprises
Shawnee Mission, Kansas 66225
Printed in the United States of America

Text and content by Steve Katz
Maps by Mike Ogden
Book design by Randy Seba
Cartoons & caricatures by Bob Bliss
Cover photographs by Ron Berry

GUIDE TO CYCLING KANSAS CITY

By
STEVE KATZ

THE COVER STORY

TABLE OF CONTENTS

Forward 4
Acknowledgements 7
History of Kansas City Cycling.................8
How to Use This Guide 10
Jackson County Area Map 13
Tour De Blue (25-28) 14
Blue Springs to Mrs. A's Restaurant (15-17) 15
Blue Springs to Mrs. A's #2 (20-22) 16
Blue Springs to Lake Tapawingo (6-8) 17
Blue Springs to Mrs. A's #3 (25+) 18
Blue Springs to Mrs. A's #4 (28-30) 19
Blue Springs to Grain Valley (20-25)..................... 20
Blue Springs to Grain Valley II (25+) 21
Blue Springs to Lakewood (25+) 22
Blue Springs to Oak Grove (30+) 23
Blue Springs to Harker's General Store (20) 24
Blue Springs to Bates City (20-25)................... 25
Blue Springs to Buckner (30-35) 26
Blue Springs to Fort Osage (35+) 27
Blue Springs to Sibley Bottoms (40+).................. 28
Johnson County Area Map 31
The Johnson County Grid 33
The Archive Ride 34
JBC Cliff Drive or City Market Rides (25) 35
Grandview Via the Back Door (40) 36
Prairie Village to Olathe (40+) 37
Prairie Village to Desoto (50) 38
Log Cabin Ride (26) 39
Prairie Village to Lee's Summit (45) 40
Prairie Village to Grandview (35) 41
The Colonel's Ride (14) 42
Kansas City Bicycle Club Welcome Ride (20) 43
Mile's Polski Day Training Ride (24) 44
75th Street Brewery Ride (17) 45
Realtor's Ride I 46
Roy's Paola Ride (40) 47
Olathe to Lawrence – A Southern Route (50)........ 48
Baldwin City Almost – Metrick (59) 49
Olathe to Ottawa (80) 50
Realtor's Ride II (Olathe) (15+) 51
Lake Olathe Ride 52
L.E.T.T.U.C.E. Ride (32/38)..............................53
Bucyrus or Bust 54
Can't Get Lost Ride (37) 55
Bill's Burrito Blast (40) 56
Tavern Ride (23) 57
Corporate Woods to the Plaza (27) 58
T.O.M.A.T.O. 59
Blue Valley Post Office to Gardner (38)..................60
Shawnee Mission Park / Wyandotte Lake (50) 61
Shwanee Mission Park to Lawrence (55) 62

TCBK – This Can't Be Kansas (55) 63
JO-29 Joyce's Tour of Shawnee (32) 64
Lenexa to Woodland Hills (28) 65
Gary Rand's 5-Hill Ride (35) 66
Lenexa to Kansas City Museum (42) 67
Lenexa to Maxine's Foods (35) 68
Northland Area Map 71
Realtor's Ride III (30)...73
Northland Show-N-GO # 1 (25)..............................74
Northland Show-N-Go # 2 (30).............................75
Boardwalk To Platte City (35+).............................76
Boardwalk To Trimble (40).....................................77
Nostalgic Interurban Ride (30)............................. 78
Mr. Mac's Annual St. Pat's Ride (44)................... 79
Airport To Faucett (60).. 80
Memorial Day Ride To Westport (26) 81
Antioch Mall To The Downtown Airport (18) 82
Northland To Cliff Drive (30)...............................83
Liberty To Platte City (50) 84
Liberty To Kearney (25) 85
Liberty To Plattsburg (53)....................................86
Liberty To Watkins Mills (42)...............................87
Smithville To Gower (58) 30 88
Smithville To Plattsburg (55)...............................89
Smithville To St. Joseph (80) 90
Excelsior Springs To Polo (60)...............................91
Plattsburg–Maysville Loop (60)............................92
Northwest Area Map 95
Bonner to Lawrence (18,36,54)............................97
Tour of Tonganoxie (43,52)..................................98
Dave's Loop (20)..99
Bi-County Loop (62)...100
Leavenworth-Wyandotte Lake (40)......................101
Roll Through Southern Platte County (32) 102
Parkville to Leavenworth (40)..............................103
Tour of Seven Cities (44).....................................104
Farley to Atchison (60) 105
Those HIlls of Missouri (40, 50)......................... 106
Leavenworth-Weston-Atchison Loop (50)............ 107
Leavenworth to Weston (25) 108
The Barn B & B Overnight (36)............................109
Nebraska and Back (44).......................................110
Easton Loop (30)..111
Winchester Loop (50) 112
Weeknite Loops (15,21).......................................113
Buffalo Bill Metric (62)......................................114
Leavenworth-Wyandotte Loop (45)......................115
Leavenworth-Tonganoxie Basehor Loop (45).......116
Leavenworth-Tonganoxie (38)..............................117
Leavenworth County Metric (62) 118
Lawrence Area Map 121

FOREWORD

Lone Star Lake (30).....................................122
Lawrence To Vinland (20).............................123
Tongnoxie Tnago (35)..................................124
Octoginta '94 (80).......................................125
Octoginta (80)..126
Lawrence To Lecompton (30).........................127
Eudora In A Round About Way (37)............128
Other Rides...129
Biking Across Kansas (BAK)........................130
Battle of Westport Ride (32)..........................131
Wheel to Weston (35, 50, 100).....................133
Bagel & Bagel Ride #1 (12)..........................134
Bagel & Bagel Ride #2.................................135
Mountain Biking 136
Mountain Biking aka Off Road Cycling.........137
Rules of the Trail..138
Bluffwoods State Forest 139
Clinton State Park 140
Hillsdale Lake..141
Indian Cave State Park.................................142
Knob Knoster State Park..............................143
Lawrence Riverfront Trail.............................144
Minor Park..145
Shawnee Mission Park.................................146
Smithville Lake 147
Weston Bend State Park 148
Bike Trails..150
The Prairie Spirit Trail 151
The Katy Trail..152
Clinton State Park 154
Tomahawk–Indian Creek Trails 155
Mill Creek Streamway & SM Park..................156
Longview Lake 157
How To Buy A Bike 158
St. Louis Bicycle Dealers..............................159
Organized Cycling......................................160
Bicycle Advocacy.......................................162
Overnight Trips..164
Bicycle Calendar..165
Bibliography`...166
Cast of Characters 167

A favorite line of mine from the Mel Brook's movie, History Of The World, is "It's good to be the king." I'm going to play king in this column and use some literary license.

Today's "information highway" and e-mail encourage readers to talk back. I don't have e-mail yet but let me hear from you:
CYCLE WRITE ENTERPRISES
P.O. BOX 26243
SHAWNEE MISSION, KS 66225
Voice Pager
(816) 426-1001
Fax
(913) 451-2192

Here are some thoughts on the following cycling subjects.

HELMETS As long as cyclists are foolish enough not to wear a helmet, the debate will continue. Do you suppose that those who don't wear helmets, also don't wear seat belts? Several friends who are accomplished cyclists claim that not to wear a helmet is their personal choice. My response is that if they had an accident while riding in the same group with me, it would ruin my day. I'd feel compelled to seek help and stay behind with them. And, if the injuries were of a lasting nature, I'd probably feel guilty I didn't convince that person to wear a helmet.

BIKE PATHS If bike paths are truly designed as bike paths, I'd have no argument. But, most trails or paths are recreational and designed to accommodate walkers, runners, on-line skaters, and sometimes cyclists. These trails give cyclists a false sense of security because of the absence of automobiles. Only a small percentage of cyclists wear helmets on trails. And, it's a fact that 2.5 times more cycling accidents occur on "bike paths" versus roads.

SIDE PATHS This is probably a foreign phrase to most readers. Bicycle advocates are constantly fighting side path legislation. A side path, much like a sidewalk, is constructed alongside a road and cyclists are required by law to use it in lieu of the road. It sounds like a good idea. A side path law is generally proposed by a legislator who has never ridden a bicycle. One such legislator in Missouri proposed that bicyclists should ride against the traffic. Simply stated, bicycles are vehicles and must be allowed to be used on all our roads and bridges

except the interstates.

BICYCLE ADVOCACY This means cyclists speaking out (lobbying) for cycling. Bicycle advocacy has been with us for over 100 years in the form of the League of American Bicyclists (LAB). As with any advocacy group, fewer than 10% do the work for the rest of us. Listed in this book are national and local bicycle advocacy groups. Find out what's underway to make our community more bicycle friendly. How can we become better at sharing the road with motorists?

BICYCLE EDUCATION
Through education, K3-12, we have a chance to make some

This book is printed on recycled paper

impression on those who will later be our adversary on the roads. Even at our most affluent elementary schools, I see kids without helmets, or helmets worn improperly, riding

in bike lanes against the traffic. Let's start volunteer bicycle programs in the schools. We could win some important battles if we can work together with our school kids and our legislators.

CHARITY RIDES A number of not-for-profit organizations use bicycle events to raise money. Many of today's Kansas City area cyclists got "turned on" to long distance cycling through the MS-150. I support the basic thesis of having fun and, at the same time, raising money. My concern is that using pledges as a way to get into the event has become tiresome. Let the charity raise the registration fee and then have an opportunity of winning prizes from raising additional funds through pledges.

I've suggested to my family that my epitaph should read, "he had both a sense of humor and a sense of history." Eleven years of cycling has given some historical perspective. The falls I've taken and the malfunctions of equipment can only be remembered with a laugh and a shake of my head. My helmet has, on at least three occasions allowed me to be here for another ride.

Good cycling,

Steve Katz

Steve Katz
CYCLE WRITE ENTERPRISES

ACKNOWLEDGMENTS

It will be stated time and time again throughout this GUIDE that this is a project by cyclists for cyclists. A very special thanks to each and every one of you. Some of you were cheerleaders, offering words of encouragement. Many are nameless cyclists who purchased my first book, Guide To Cycling Kansas City. Others of you provided the maps and routes without which this guide would not have been possible. When I first decided to compile this current edition, I invited about 25 cyclists to my home -- and 27 showed up. With so many many people to whom we're indebted, it's possible we have inadvertently left out some names. Please forgive the oversight and consider yourself an important part of this book.

Chuck Battey III
Gene & Thelma Dreyer
Tom & Dot Thomas
Bill Maasen-Johnson County Parks
Marlene Nagel - MARC

Lynn McGivern
Nancy Diehl
Jim & Joyce Kaplan
Tim Osburn
Dave Van Wyck
Art Loepp

Phil Harris
Marsha & Dan Thompson
Jim Bretz
Buzz O'Brian
Larry Perry

Carroll Denning
Pat Coffman
Bev Chapman
Dennis Jones
T.J. Bergner

Ed & Nancy Proctor
Steve & Chris Edmonds
Roy & Anna Antoki
John West - Hillsdale
Darrel Hunter
Gene & Becky Napier

Dick & Emily Ballentine
Steve Forsyth & Sharon Coberly
Billie & John Owen
Glen Shepard
Mahlon Strahm

Front cover:
Mike McCrary
Bonnie Phelan
John Harris
Stuart Bitner

Mo Dept of Forestry:
John Fleming
Mark Nelson
Ruth Sotak
Henry Meyer
Ron Berry

Jim Turner
Laurie Scrutchfield
Dan & Bar Beatty
Dick & Carol Stephens
Larry Stanfield
Joyce Thompson
Jim Burruss
Don Inbody

This book is dedicated to my daughters, Jennifer and Laura. Your encouragement and your support were there when I needed it most. And, to my wife, Lynda, when she broke her leg on our honeymoon, I gained a wife but lost the stoker on my tandem.

7

HISTORY OF KANSAS CITY CYCLING

The earliest name in Kansas City cycling to be found was Carl Schutte, founder of Schutte Lumber. Schutte was an Olympic medalist in cycling in 1912.

A look at the development of cycling in America gives us a better understanding of cycling popularity in Kansas City. The League of American (LAW), which only recently changed it's name to the League of American Bicyclists (LAB), is the nation's first and oldest bicycle advocacy group. This organization was founded in the 1880's to fight for cyclists' rights. The 1890's were considered the golden age of cycling. At that time the League boasted nearly 100,000 members.

But, the success of the League's Good Roads Campaign, together with the advent of automobiles and trolleys, brought about the decline in the popularity of the bicycle.

Manufacturers and consumers alike came to consider the bicycle as a toy rather than a means of transportation, an attitude that would prevail until the Great Depression. Except for an occasional paper boy or a telegraph messenger boy, bicycles became the province of the kids.

During the early 1900's when Carl Schutte won his Olympic medal, only a few hard core cyclists competed. Cycling, as a means of transportation in both Kansas City and the U.S., experienced only brief upturns during World Ward II and during the energy crisis of the 1970's.

Kansas Citian, Henry Meyer participated in track racing in and around the Kansas City area beginning in 1933. Another competitor, Henry recalled, was Bob Falderman. Both men participated in six day bicycle races held In the old Municipal Auditorium. Henry Meyer recalled that in those days it wasn't unusual to pass an automobile on a bicycle.

In the post World War II era, an Air Force Colonel named Stith led The Colonel's Ride on Sunday. Even today, this weekly Sunday tradition still starts from Loose Park and generally attracts more than 100 riders.

In about 1963, the Kansas City Bicycle Club (KCBC) was formed. Much later other clubs like the Johnson County Bicycle Club (JCBC) came along. Each club sponsored an annual ride. In 1969 the Octoginta classic started in Lawrence, Kansas, and today is sponsored by the Lawrence Bicycle Club.

WOW (Women On Wheels) started in the early 1970's as a Tuesday morning ride from Waid's in Prairie Village. The group consisted of Carol Weingarden Hummel, Marianne Hahn, Imogene Thiessen, Alice Lavender, and Evelyn Frohmberg.

Shakespeare said, "What's past is prologue." It's difficult to know in which direction we're headed without knowing first where we've been. The tradition of Kansas City cycling coupled with the awareness and concern of our advocates should insure that the future is a bright one. New trails including The KATY Trail and the Prairie Spirit Trail and designated mountain bike areas create recreation and transportation venues for all members of the family to enjoy.

HOW TO USE THIS GUIDE

Guide to Cycling Kansas City is copyrighted. *Each map and graphic as it appears in this Guide is the property of Cycle Write Enterprises.* Because of this Guide's size and format, we're aware that carrying it on your bicycle is a weighty problem.

Therefore, we encourage you to copy individual maps for your own personal use and enjoyment. Mark or highlight the maps for difficult passages. We'd just like to avoid seeing reproductions of the Guide or even sections of it for commercial use.

Where To Look For Information
The Guide is divided into 6 sections:

⟶ Jackson County

⟶ Johnson County

⟶ Northland

⟶ Leavenworth & Northwest

⟶ Lawrence

⟶ Other... Trails & Offroad

The starting point of a ride determines into which sector a ride is placed. For example, a ride starting in Prairie Village and going to Lee's Summit with 75% of the ride in Jackson County is, nevertheless, a Johnson County ride.

Safety
Since almost all rides are on public roads, the Guide defers the responsibility for your safety to you. Obviously, conditions for any given ride vary with the wether, the traffic, the day of the week, and the time of the day.

Meeting Other Cyclists
If you happen to be an inexperienced cyclist or new to the area, we would urge you to join one of the cycling organizations listed on page and to try an organized ride. In addition to the Bike Clubs, we have included a listing of Bicycle Dealers to aid in purchasing a new bicycle or in servicing the one you already own. These bicycle shops are both capable and willing to suggest routes to try and organizations to join.

Expanding Horizons
Most cyclists tend to "ride in their own backyard." We suggest you use this Guide to explore other areas. On page there's a list of organized rides for every day of the week. This is an excellent way to learn new routes and to meet new people.

New Features
We've added a number of new features to this book. Probably the most important is the section on off road cycling and bike trails. Please read and heed our comments at the start of each of these sections.

We hope the Guide To Cycling Kansas City will become your passport to new, adventuresome, and exciting bicycling in the Kansas City, Lawrence, and Leavenworth areas.

JIM
BRETZ

rides with his head as well as his heart. The portion of this book on eastern Jackson County is 100% the work of Jim Bretz. The devotion to cycling of Jim Bretz was a motivating factor in the completion of this book.

DAN
BEATTY

It would be impossible to talk Kansas City cycling without mentioning Dan Beatty. He started cycling in the 1970s and by the end of the decade was a noted local authority on bicycle repairs. Dan met his wife, Barb, on BAK '87 and they have been a pair ever since. Much of their riding today is tandem.

Page

1. Tour De Blue (25-28) 14

2. Blue Springs to Mrs. A's Restaurant (15-17).........15

3. Blue Springs to Mrs. A's #2 (20-22) 16

4. Blue Springs to Lake Tapawingo (6-8).................17

5. Blue Springs to Mrs. A's #3 (25+) 18

6. Blue Springs to Mrs. A's #4 (28-30) 19

7. Blue Springs to Grain Valley (20-25)................... 20

8. Blue Springs to Grain Valley II (25+) 21

9. Blue Springs to Lakewood (25+) 22

10. Blue Springs to Oak Grove (30+)........................23

11. Blue Springs to Harker's General Store (20-25)...24

12. Blue Springs to Bates City (20-25)...................... 25

13. Blue Springs to Buckner (30-35) 26

14. Blue Springs to Fort Osage (35+)....................... 27

15. Blue Springs to Sibley Bottoms (40+) 28

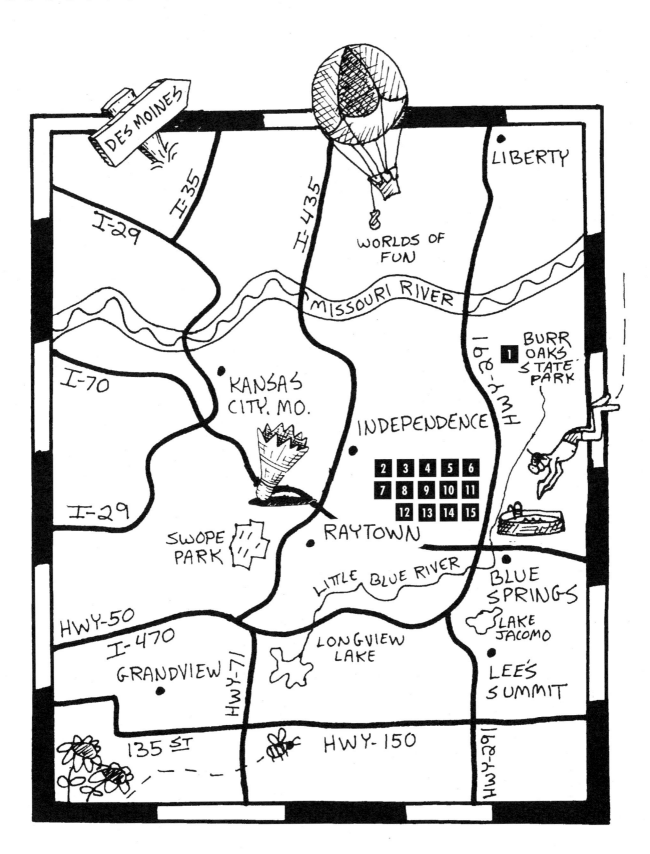

13

TOUR DE BLUE

Starting Point: Pink Hill Park, on Hwy 7 a mile and a half north of I-70, left on park Rd at James Lewis Elementary School.

Distance: 25-28 miles (all in Blue Springs)

Things To See: Sights include a Gray Line tour of scenic Blue Springs, hence the ride name. Also, Waterfield, Lake Tapawingo, and Blue Springs Park.

So we're not beholden to anyone, there are several good places to eat. Ride by Jim Bretz.

Warm up and jockey for position by circling baseball fields. RIGHT on Park Road into Burr Oaks. Improvise through the park, then ride east on Park Rd to Hwy 7

LEFT on Hwy 7

RIGHT at Hunter

LEFT at 4th Terrace, continue as it turns into 3rd Terrace

LEFT again on 4th Terrace and up the hill

LEFT on Roanoak

RIGHT on Adams Dairy Rd

LEFT into Waterfield and circle this housing addition

Exit and RIGHT on Duncan

LEFT at Adam's Dairy

RIGHT at Country Club, across Hwy 7, to Outer Road

LEFT on R.D. Mize, over I-70, then called Woods Chapel, to entrance Lake Tapawingo

RIGHT and counter clockwise around lake (3+ miles) obeying local laws.

Exit lake with RIGHT onto Woods Chapel

LEFT on Walnut, up hill, past Methodist Church, and cemetery

RIGHT on 25th

Left at South Avenue through Blue Springs Park

RIGHT at 19th Street, across Hwy 40

LEFT at Clark

LEFT on Luttrell to Hwy 40 and Mickey D's

RIGHT on Hwy 40, across 7, under railroad bridge

LEFT at Moore

RIGHT on Sunnyside, across R.D. Mize, to Mock

RIGHT on Hwy 7

LEFT at Park Road to starting point

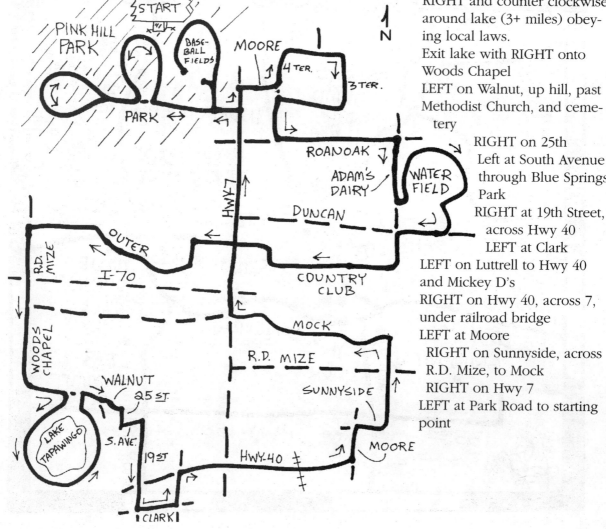

BLUE SPRINGS TO MRS A'S RESTAURANT

Starting Point: Blue Springs Centennial Pool Plex, 22nd Street, Blue Springs
Distance: 15-17 miles
Degree of Difficulty: easy
Terrain: friendly
Things To See: Independence "International" Airport and Mrs. A's Restaurant

A relatively short and easy beginners ride says Jim Bretz. Start from the swimming pool because it's easy to find and the parking is good. From the pool parking lot
LEFT to Outer Road
LEFT to Woods Chapel
RIGHT across I-70 and you're now on R.D. Mize
CONTINUE across 39th, by the fire station, down a big hill to Mrs. A's Restaurant

After a breakfast of the Airport or Runway Special, return to R.D. Mize Road
RIGHT about 1/4 mile to Selsa Road
LEFT on Selsa Road across tracks, across 39th, over I-70 around the corner, past the soccer fields to the first street that goes left across from Tri-City Ministries.
LEFT to Valley View
LEFT on Valley View, past the park, up the hill, past the school, up the hill to 37th St.
RIGHT on Briarwood to Woods Chapel
Cross Woods Chapel - now on Kingsridge
Kingsridge to 22nd Street and the pool (and hopefully your car)

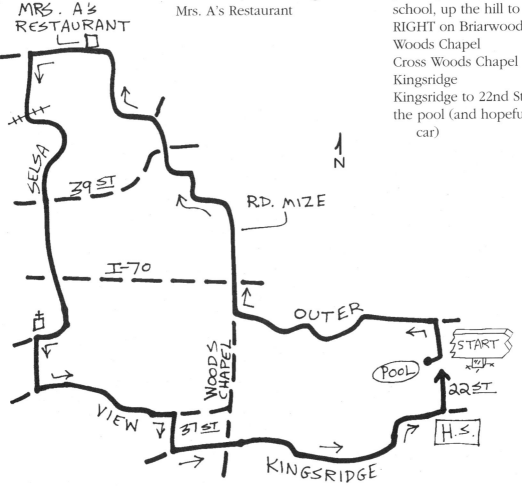

BLUE SPRINGS TO MRS A'S #2

Starting Point: Blue Springs Centennial Pool Plex, 22nd Street, Blue Springs
Distance: 20-22 miles
Degree of Difficulty: Fairly easy
Terrain: moderate hills
Things To See: extra loop past MCI Hospital and Mrs. A's Restaurant at Independence Airport

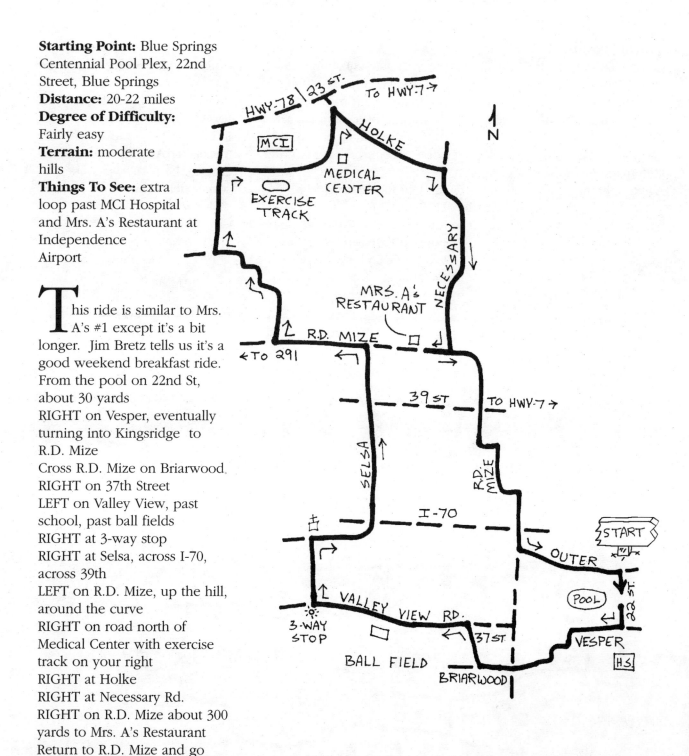

This ride is similar to Mrs. A's #1 except it's a bit longer. Jim Bretz tells us it's a good weekend breakfast ride. From the pool on 22nd St, about 30 yards
RIGHT on Vesper, eventually turning into Kingsridge to R.D. Mize
Cross R.D. Mize on Briarwood.
RIGHT on 37th Street
LEFT on Valley View, past school, past ball fields
RIGHT at 3-way stop
RIGHT at Selsa, across I-70, across 39th
LEFT on R.D. Mize, up the hill, around the curve
RIGHT on road north of Medical Center with exercise track on your right
RIGHT at Holke
RIGHT at Necessary Rd.
RIGHT on R.D. Mize about 300 yards to Mrs. A's Restaurant
Return to R.D. Mize and go LEFT, up the hill, across 39th St., across I-70
LEFT (careful) on Outer Road
RIGHT on 22nd to the starting point

BLUE SPRINGS TO LAKE TAPAWINGO

Starting Point: Blue Springs Centennial Pool Plex, 22nd Street, Blue Springs
Distance: 6-8 miles
Degree of Difficulty: short and easy
Terrain: friendly
Things To See: Lake Tapawingo, respect the locals and the law, be careful of traffic within Blue Springs city limits.

From pool RIGHT on 22nd Street
LEFT on Ashton
RIGHT at 15th, across railroad bridge
RIGHT at Vesper down the hill, up a short hill, and past the park
LEFT on R.D. Mize about 20 yards to Lake Tapawingo entrance.
RIGHT around lake counter-clockwise; cycle the loop as many times as time permits.
Exit Lake Tapawingo and stay left on R.D. Mize
RIGHT on Kingsridge back to pool

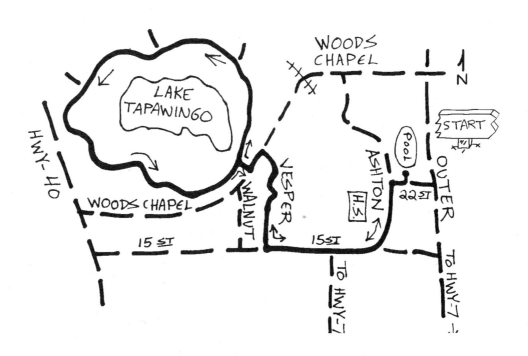

Starting Point: Blue Springs Centennial Pool plex, 22nd Street, Blue Springs
Distance: 25+ miles
Degree of Difficulty: challenging
Terrain: somewhat hilly
Things To See: when it's hilly we don't enjoy the scenery as much. Mrs. A's Restaurant is a welcome repast

From the pool cycle left on 22nd Street
LEFT on Outer Rd.
RIGHT at Woods Chapel, across I-70
RIGHT at Crenshaw Rd.
LEFT on Truman Rd.
LEFT on Highway 78
LEFT at Holke Rd.
LEFT at R.D. Mize to Mrs. A's Restaurant
Return RIGHT on R.D. Mize
LEFT on Selsa, across 39th, over I-70 to road across from Tri-City ministires
LEFT on Valley View to 37th
RIGHT at 37th
LEFT at Briarwood, across Wood Chapel (now Kingsridge) to the starting point.

BLUE SPRINGS TO MRS. A'S #4

Starting Point: Blue Springs Centennial Pool plex, 22nd Street, Blue Springs
Distance: 28—30 miles
Degree of Difficulty: somewhat difficult
Terrain: some hills especially on Truman Road
Things To See: good ride early morning on a weekend.

Jim Bretz calls this "the 4th variation on the Ode To Grease theme." When you've completed four rides to Mrs. A's, you'll be on a first name basis. Time to have your cholesterol checked.

LEFT from pool on 22nd St.
RIGHT on Outer Road
LEFT at Hwy 7
RIGHT at Pink Hill Road (5th stoplight)

LEFT on Dillingham
LEFT on Truman Road for serious hills
RIGHT at Hwy 7 for about 300 dangerous yards
LEFT at Truman Road
LEFT on Hwy 78
LEFT on Holke Rd., behind MCI
LEFT at R.D. Mize to Mrs. A's Restaurant
Return LEFT on R.D. Mize
LEFT on Outer Road (be careful)
RIGHT on 22nd St. to starting point

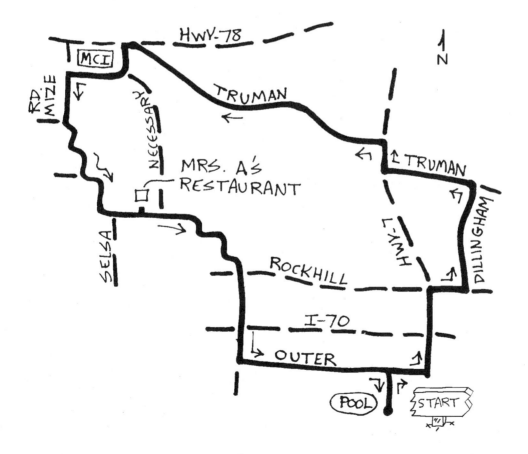

BLUE SPRINGS TO GRAIN VALLEY

Starting Point: Blue Springs Centennial Pool plex, 22nd Street, Blue Springs
Distance: 20-25 miles
Degree of Difficulty: easy
Terrain: some hills on R.D. Mize and AA

For those who need a change from Mrs. A's, there's Pilot Truck Stop in Grain Valley for snacks and ice cream next door. Gourmet cyclists can try Mickey D's at intersection of Mock and Hwy 7.

LEFT on 22nd Street
RIGHT on Outer Road, across Hwy 7 with Mickey D on left becomes Mock
LEFT at R.D. Mize
LEFT at Hwy 40 to BB (Buckner Tarnsey Rd). Pilot Truck Stop at Hwy 40 and BB City Park is 1/4 mile south on BB
Follow BB through town, across tracks
RIGHT on AA
RIGHT on Hwy 40. Watch for fast moving traffic.
LEFT at Moore
RIGHT on Sunnyside School, across R.D. Mize (now Mock), across Hwy 7
LEFT on 22nd Street

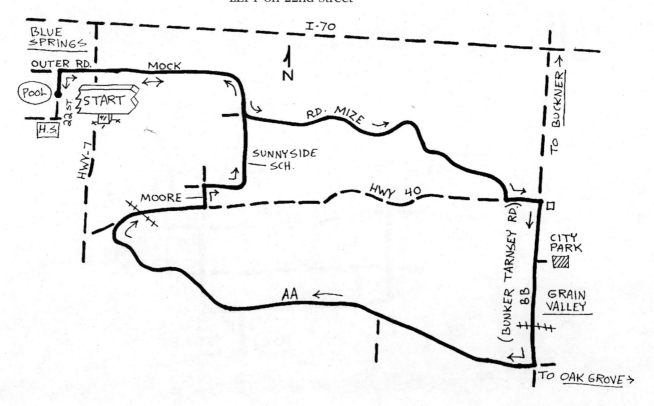

BLUE SPRINGS TO GRAIN VALLEY II

Starting Point: Blue Springs Centennial Pool plex, 22nd Street, Blue Springs
Distance: 25+ miles
Degree of Difficulty: a good workout
Terrain: a few hills
Things To See: This is truly a country ride.

Food options are limited with Mickey D's one of them.

RIGHT on 22nd Street
LEFT on Vesper
RIGHT at 15th
LEFT at Walnut
RIGHT on 10th, across Hwy 40
LEFT on Clark, across Hwy 7, becoming Keystone Drive
LEFT at 2nd
LEFT at Shamrock

RIGHT on 1st Street
LEFT on Moreland School
RIGHT at Cook (watch the hill)
LEFT at Major Road
LEFT on Arnette, down Minter Hill
RIGHT on AA to BB and Grain Valley
LEFT on BB to Pilot Truck Stop
LEFT at Yennie to Hwy 40
LEFT at Moore
RIGHT on Sunnyside School, across R.D. Mize to Mock, and across Hwy 7
LEFT on 22nd Street and back to starting point

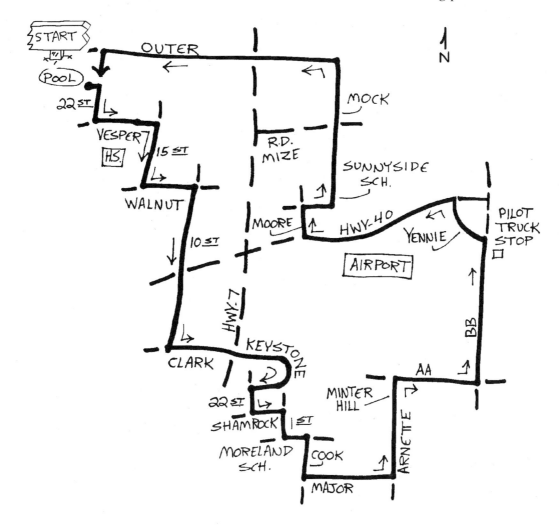

BLUE SPRINGS TO LAKEWOOD

Starting Point: Blue Springs Centennial Pool plex, 22nd Street, Blue Springs
Distance: 25+
Degree of Difficulty: not very
Terrain: mostly flat
Things To See: Lakewood is an upscale community with a lake, golfing, and beautiful homes.

For food, there's a Quik Trip at Lakewood entrance, Mrs. A's on R.D. Mize, McDonald's at Outer Rd and Woods Chapel, and Perkins at Outer Rd and Hwy 7.

Cycle right on 22nd St
RIGHT on Vesper, across Woods Chapel, now called Briarwood
RIGHT on 37th
LEFT at Valley View
RIGHT at 3-way stop
LEFT on Selsa, across Hwy 40
LEFT on Lakewood Way
RIGHT at Fairview
RIGHT at T intersection
LEFT on Lakewood Way
RIGHT on Bowlin Rd into Lakewood Quik-Trip
Take Bowlin across dam
LEFT at Lake Drive

LEFT at Gregory, across 291
LEFT on Outer Road north across Bowlin Rd, Hwy 40, becomes Selsa
RIGHT on R.D. Mize Rd, across I-70
LEFT at Outer Rd
RIGHT at 22nd and back to start

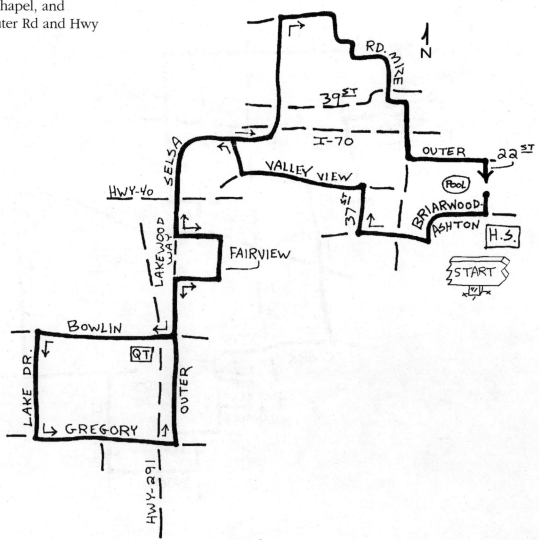

BLUE SPRINGS TO OAK GROVE

Starting Point: Blue Springs Centennial Pool plex, 22nd Street, Blue Springs
Distance: 30+ miles
Degree of Difficulty: fairly easy
Things To See: back road to Oak Grove; at least two places to eat in Oak Grove, Jack's and MacDonald's.

Cycle right on 22nd St
LEFT on Ashton
RIGHT at 15th
LEFT at Walnut across Hwy 7
RIGHT on 4th St.
LEFT on Chicago
RIGHT at Moore
LEFT at Hwy 40, to first exit past airport
RIGHT on Yennie

RIGHT on BB to AA
Cycle old US 40 across several bridges and up some hills
RIGHT at Outer Rd.
RIGHT at H (Oak Grove) & MacDonalds
RIGHT on H, across I-70, about 3 miles to blinkin light
LEFT on Pink Hill Road to BB
LEFT on Hwy 7 either under I-70 or cut through Amoco
RIGHT at Outer Rd.
LEFT at 22nd St.

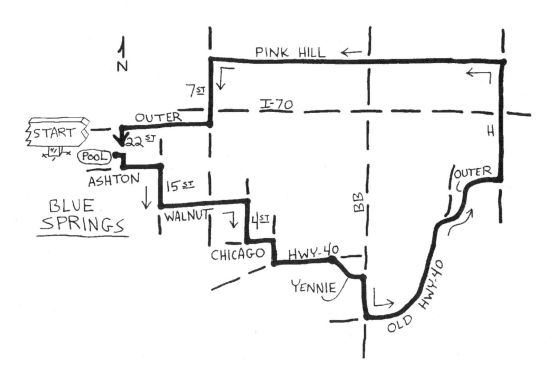

BLUE SPRINGS TO HARKER'S GENERAL STORE

Starting Point: Blue Springs Centennial Pool plex, 22nd Street, Blue Springs
Distance: 20-25 miles
Degree of Difficulty: not a problem
Terrain: mostly flat
Things To See: an old style general store with a front porch and even rocking chairs.

Cycle right on 22nd St.
LEFT on Ashton
RIGHT at 15th
LEFT at Walnut
RIGHT on 10th across Hwy 40
LEFT on Clark across Hwy 7 to Keystone Dr.
LEFT at 2nd St.
LEFT at Shamrock
RIGHT on 1st
LEFT on Moreland School Rd.
RIGHT at Cook
RIGHT at Wyatt
LEFT on Shrout
LEFT on Colbern
RIGHT at BB and Harker's
Return with LEFT on Colbern
RIGHT at Litchford
RIGHT at Cook
LEFT on Moreland School
RIGHT on 1st
LEFT at Shamrock
RIGHT at 2nd
RIGHT on Keystone across Hwy 7, to Clark
RIGHT on Luttrell across Hwy 40 becoming 10th St.
LEFT at Walnut
RIGHT at 15th
LEFT on Ashton
RIGHT on 22nd to the pool.

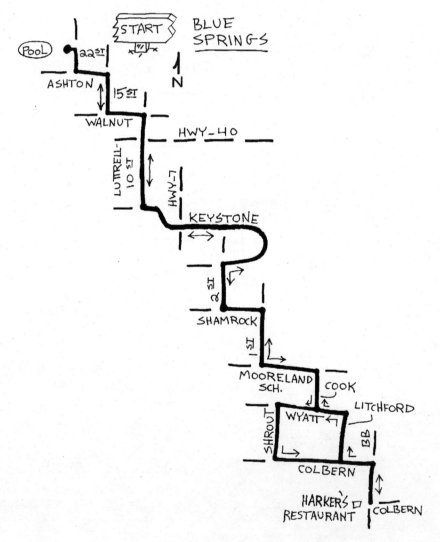

BLUE SPRINGS TO BATES CITY

Starting Point: Blue Springs Centennial Pool plex, 22nd Street, Blue Springs
Distance: 30-35 miles
Degree of Difficulty: a little difficult
Terrain: a few hills
Things To See: Bates City Bar-B-Que, MacDonald's in Oak Grove

Cycle right on 22nd St.
LEFT on Ashton
RIGHT at 15th
LEFT in Walnut across Hwy 7
RIGHT at 4th St.
LEFT on Chicago
RIGHT on Moore
LEFT at Hwy 40 to Grain Valley and Yennie
RIGHT at Yennie
RIGHT on BB to AA/Old Hwy 40
LEFT on Old Hwy 40 to Rte H and Grain Valley
Outer Road to Bates City - Bates City BBQ is on Z, about 1/2 mile, by railroad tracks. After BBQ, return to Outer Road and cycle right to Rte D
LEFT at Rte D, across I-70
LEFT at FF
LEFT on Rte H
RIGHT on Pink Hill (blinker light)
LEFT at Hwy 7 under I-70
RIGHT at Outer Rd.
LEFT on 22nd St. to pool.

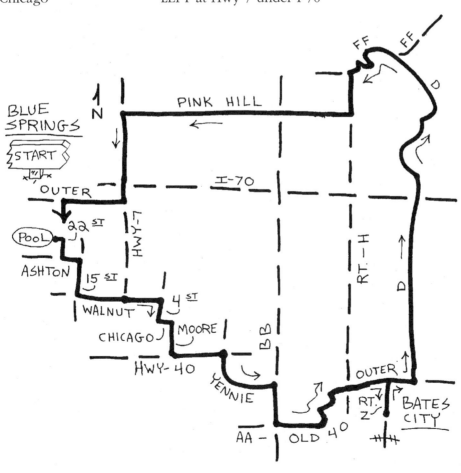

BLUE SPRINGS TO BUCKNER

Starting Point: Blue Springs Centennial Pool
plex, 22nd Street, Blue Springs
Distance: 30-35 miles
Degree of Difficulty: not much
Terrain: good "cruising roads" with one nasty
hill
Things To See:

RIGHT on 22nd St.
LEFT on Outer Road
RIGHT at Woods
Chapel Rd. across
I-70
RIGHT at Crenshaw
LEFT on Truman Rd
RIGHT on Hwy 78
North at Hwy 7 (traffic cir-
cle) counter clockwise
RIGHT at Bundschu
RIGHT on Elsie Smith
LEFT on Heidelberger
across tracks
Lake City-Buckner (a great
road)
LEFT at Central, across the tracks, to
intersection of Hwy 24 and the New
Wave
Return by the same route.

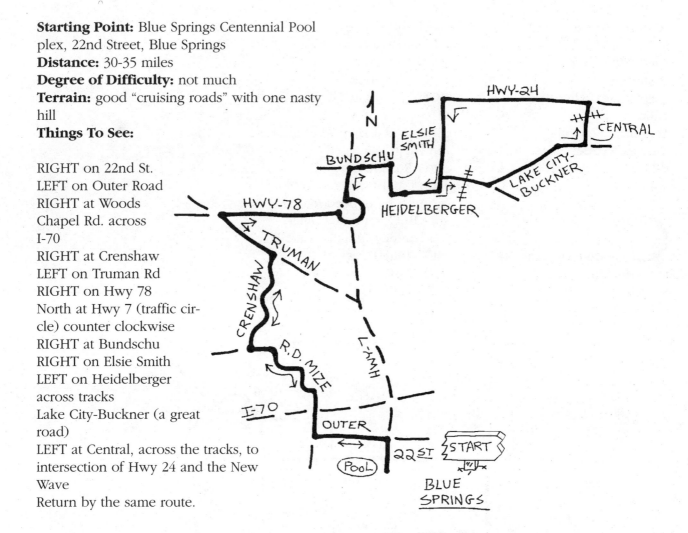

BLUE SPRINGS TO FORT OSAGE

Starting Point: Blue Springs Centennial Pool plex, 22nd Street, Blue Springs

Distance: 35+ miles

Degree of Difficulty: rather easy

Terrain: rolling

Things To See: Old Fort Osage trading post; good picnic ride;

Eat at New Wave and a restaurant at intersection of Hwy 24 and BB

Cycle left on 22nd St.
LEFT on Outer Rd.
RIGHT at Woods Chapel across I-70
RIGHT at Crenshaw
LEFT on Truman Rd.
RIGHT on Hwy 78 to traffic circle, counter clockwise and north on Hwy 7
RIGHT at Bundschu
RIGHT at Elsie Smith
LEFT on Heidelberger over tracks
LEFT on Lake City-Buckner
LEFT at BB across Hwy 24 which is then Blue Mills, up hill
RIGHT at Buckner-Tarsney
LEFT on Chicago
RIGHT at first intersection (unmarked road)

RIGHT at Falconer to the Fort.
Return on Falconer
LEFT on unmarked road
LEFT at Chicago
RIGHT at Buckner-Tarnsey
RIGHT on Blue Mills
LEFT on Elsie Smith
RIGHT at Bundschu
LEFT at Hwy 7
RIGHT on Hwy 78
LEFT on Truman
RIGHT at Crenshaw
LEFT at R.D. Mize across I-70
LEFT on Outer Rd.
RIGHT on 22nd to the Blue Springs pool

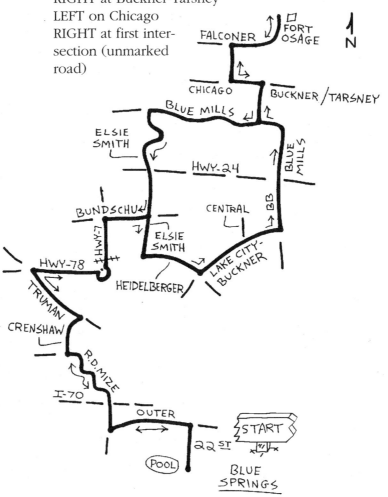

BLUE SPRINGS TO SIBLEY BOTTOMS

Starting Point: Blue Springs Centennial Pool plex, 22nd Street, Blue Springs
Distance: 40+ miles
Degree of Difficulty: challenging
Terrain: few hills
Things To See: rural scenery; New Wave restaurant in Buckner

Cycle from Blue Springs pool
LEFT on 22nd St.
RIGHT on Outer Rd.
LEFT at Hwy 7
RIGHT at Pink Hill Road
LEFT on Kirby
LEFT on FF
RIGHT at Little
LEFT at Sunny Nook
LEFT on Mabry Road
RIGHT on Airport
LEFT at Old 24
RIGHT at BB, across Hwy 24, becoming Blue Mills Rd.
RIGHT on Koger Rd.
LEFT on Atherton-Sibley Road
LEFT at Old Atherton, not marked, so look for sign "Independence"
LEFT across RR tracks
LEFT at Blue Mills to Little Blue Trace Park and bike trail.
RIGHT on Hwy 78
LEFT on Truman Rd.
RIGHT at Crenshaw, up the hill
LEFT at R.D. Mize
LEFT on Outer Road
RIGHT on 22nd back to pool

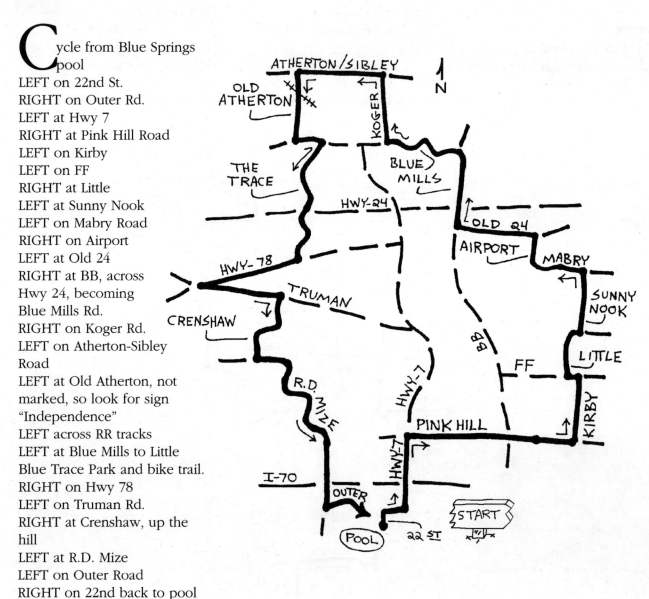

MIKE BLASER

is a person who it's difficult to say anything about that hasn't already been said. Mike took up cycling in 1964 because he needed "a place to sit down." Many of his rides have something to do with food. Mike Blaser is always game for a new and unusual ride as long as it's challenging.

JOYCE THOMPSON

is the resident expert on the Shawnee area. Joyce began seriously cycling in 1982. She and her husband, Wayne, trained and rode BAK. Joyce is a dominant force behind efforts to improve cycling in our communities. Joyce is totally involved in anything and everything she does. "Advocate" best describes Joyce Thompson.

Page

1. The Johnson County Grid.............................33
2. The Archive Ride 34
3. JBC Cliff Drive or City Market Rides (25) 35
4. Grandview Via the Back Door (40) 36
5. Prairie Village to Olathe (40+).............................37
6. Prairie Village to Desoto (50) 38
7. Log Cabin Ride (26)....................................... 39
8. Prairie Village to Lee's Summit (45) 40
9. Prairie Village to Grandview (35) 41
10. The Colonel's Ride (14) 42
11. Kansas City Bicycle Club Welcome Ride (20) 43
12. Mile's Polski Day Training Ride (24).......................44
13. 75th Street Brewery Ride (17) 45
14. Realtor's Ride I 46
15. Roy's Paola Ride (40)................................. 47
16. Olathe to Lawrence – A Southern Route (50) 48
17. Baldwin City Almost – Metrick (59)........................ 49
18. Olathe to Ottawa (80)................................ 50
19. Realtor's Ride II (Olathe) (15+) 51
20. Lake Olathe Ride 52
21. L.E.T.T.U.C.E. Ride (32/38) 53
22. Bucyrus or Bust 54
23. Can't Get Lost Ride (37)................................55
24. Bill's Burrito Blast (40)...............................56
25. Tavern Ride (23).....................................57
26. Corporate Woods to the Plaza (27)........................58
27. T.O.M.A.T.O. 59
28. Blue Valley Post Office to Gardner (38) 60
29. Shawnee Mission Park to Wyandotte Lake (50)........61
30. Shwanee Mission Park to Lawrence (55)...................62
31. TCBK – This Can't Be Kansas (55)........................63
32. JO-29 Joyce's Tour of Shawnee (32)......................64
33. Lenexa to Woodland Hills (28)..........................65
34. Gary Rand's 5-Hill Ride (35)...........................66
35. Lenexa to Kansas City Museum (42)....................67
36. Lenexa to Maxine's Foods (35) 68

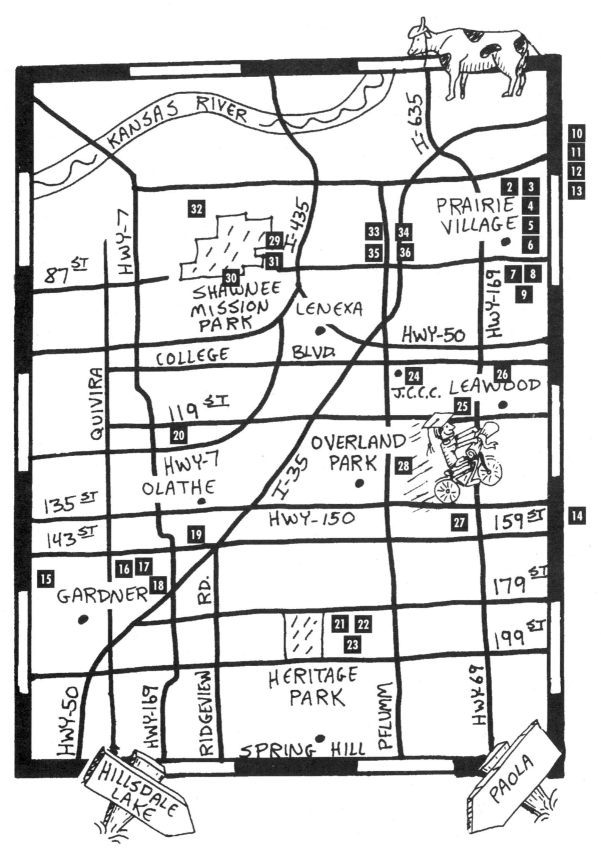

KANSAS RIVER

I-635

32

I-435

PRAIRIE
VILLAGE

10
11
12
13

2 3
4
5
6

33 34

35 36

29

31

30

87 ST

HWY-7

SHAWNEE
MISSION
PARK

LENEXA

HWY-169

7 8
9

COLLEGE   BLVD.

HWY-50

QUIVIRA

119 ST

24

J.C.C.C. LEAWOOD

26

20

25

HWY-7

OLATHE

OVERLAND
PARK

I-35

28

135 ST

143 ST

19

HWY-150

27

159 ST

14

15

16 17

18

GARDNER

RD.

179 ST

199 ST

21 22

23

RIDGEVIEW

HERITAGE
PARK

PFLUMM

HWY-169

HWY-50

HWY-169

SPRING HILL

HILLSDALE
LAKE

PAOLA

31

LARRY STANFIELD

started cycling when he decided to "do one last thing before his son turned 16 and got a car." Larry did the first MS-150 and has done every one since. He's the self-elected president of the Bungee Bike Club. This idea came to him when he was struggling up a hill and someone passed, smiled, and said "have a nice day."

GLEN SHEPARD

is a person who knows no limits. Glen always attempts to cycle further and faster than he has before. In recent years he's successfully attempted two ultra distance cycling events - Paris-Brest-Brest and Boston-Montreal-Boston. Glen's enthusiasm for everything he does is contagious. His positive attitude and support were major factors in the completion of this book.

JOHNSON COUNTY GRID

This Johnson County Grid was an idea long before the revision of this book. I thought it would be a simple plan to put together and north-south, east-west grid of roads in Johnson County south of 119th Street.

On further examination, I found my old favorites of College Blvd and 119th Street to be totally impassable on a bicycle. The north-south roads that are paved and passable are another matter all together.

I engaged the services of realtor and cyclist Dick Stephens who managed to make some sense out of this chaos. This map is, for the moment, those roads that might be routes you can cycle. There might be some criticism, but nothing ventured, nothing gained.

DICK STEPHENS

has integrated cycling into his very successful real estate business. Those who ride southern Johnson County are frequently reminded of Dick Stephens by his name on real estate signs. He cycles to stay healthy and to enjoy the company of others.

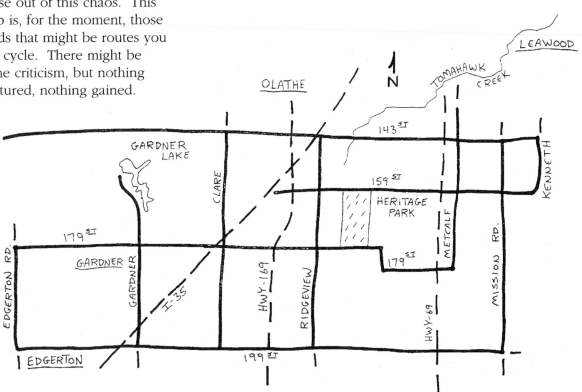

THE ARCHIVE RIDE

Starting Point: Waid's Restaurant, Prairie Village Shopping Center
Distance: 20 miles
Degree of Difficulty: easy as finding some lost relative
Terrain: flat
Things To See: Kansas City is home to one of several regional offices of the National Archives. If you have any interest in your family history, take this ride and acquaint yourself with this remarkable facility located at 3312 E. Bannister Rd. next to the IRS. Office hours are 8-4 Monday thru Friday and 9-4 the 3rd Saturday of the month. Specific information can be obtained by calling (816) 926-6272.

RIGHT on The Paseo south thru Marborough area across 85th St.
Continue south through Legacy Park and through a gate to large industrial complex.
Inside gate cycle east (left) through parking lots to northeast end of complex where Archives are located.
When leaving cycle south from Archives past IRS
LEFT at 95th St.
RIGHT almost immediately on access road to Blue River Pkwy.
OPTION to cycle right on Blue River Pkwy and follow it south to Blue Ridge Blvd.
LEFT (north) on Blue River Parkway

LEFT on Grandview Rd. across Blue River
Continue across 85th becoming Prospect
LEFT at top of hill 81st St
RIGHT at Brooklyn to top of short hill
LEFT on 80th St
RIGHT on The Paseo
LEFT on 80th and west across Troost becoming 79th Terr. continuing across Holmes
RIGHT on Grand and continue north across Gregory
LEFT at 70th Terrace
RIGHT at Brookside
LEFT on 70th
RIGHT on Pennsylvania
LEFT at 69th St. and west across Ward Pkwy, State Line, Belinder, into Prairie Village

This ride can only be done on weekdays. The Archives are closed except on the 3rd Saturday and the north entrance gate to the complex is locked on weekends.
Cycle east from Prairie Village S.C. on 69th St. across State Line and Ward Parkway
RIGHT at Pennsylvania
LEFT at 70th across Wornall
RIGHT on Brookside
LEFT at 70th Terrace
RIGHT at Cherry
LEFT on Gregory across Troost

JCBC CLIFF DRIVE....OR CITY MARKET RIDES

Starting Point: Prairie Village Shopping Center, 69th & Mission Rd

Distance: 25 miles

Degree of Difficulty: not a problem

Terrain: mostly flat except return from river

Things To See: A Sunday kind of ride, with option to see the City Market instead

Cycle from Prairie Village on 69th St
LEFT at Valley which becomes Summit about 61st St
RIGHT at 51st at north end of Loose Park
LEFT on Main St
RIGHT at Grand entrance to Crown Center
OPTION to continue straight into City Market (return south on Grand, right on Linwood, left at Broadway, right at Westport, and left on Mission Rd) Randy:box this
RIGHT on 5th St
RIGHT on Cherry
LEFT at Independence
LEFT at Maple
RIGHT on Cliff Drive always staying to left and clockwise around lake
Return from Cliff Drive with LEFT on Maple

RIGHT at Independence
LEFT at Charlotte
RIGHT on Linwood
LEFT on Broadway
RIGHT at Westport
LEFT at Mission Road to Prairie Village

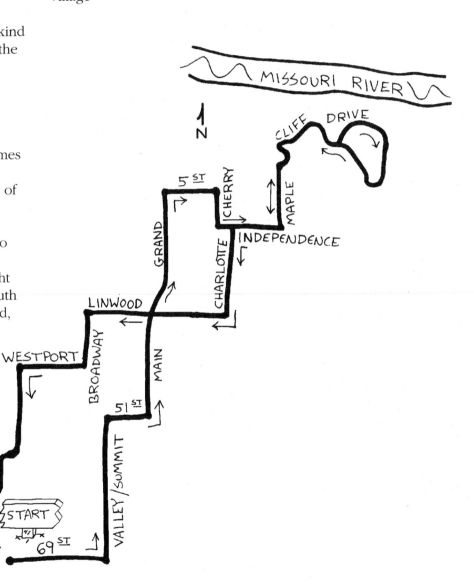

35

GRANDVIEW VIA THE BACK DOOR

Starting Point: Waid's Restaurant, Tomahawk & Mission, Prairie Village
Distance: 40 miles
Degree of Difficulty: fairly easy
Terrain: gently rolling, and fast on Blue River pkwy
Things To See: popular Tuesday morning ride for "retirees;" breakfast at Oden's Restaurant, 127th & 71 Hwy in Grandview; scenic and fast return through Minor Park on Blue River Pkwy.

Cycle from Waid's southwest on Tomahawk Rd
RIGHT on Ash
LEFT at 73rd St
LEFT at Nall across 75th St
RIGHT on Tomahawk
LEFT on Dearborn across 79th and up a hill
Becomes Woodson at 83rd St
RIGHT at 87th Terrace
LEFT on Horton across 91st (with extreme caution)
Stay left on Outlook across 95th becomes Horton across 103rd
RIGHT at Indian Creek Drive
LEFT at Lamar and continue south across College
LEFT on 115th
RIGHT on Nall
LEFT at 119th St
RIGHT at Rosewood
LEFT on Tomahawk Creek Pkwy
RIGHT on Roe south across 135th (Hwy 150) (extreme caution)
LEFT at 138th (Leawood Meadows) winding east to

Mission Rd
RIGHT at Mission
LEFT on 151st St past 4-way stop on Kenneth Rd (State Line)
Continue east uphill to Holmes
RIGHT on Holmes
LEFT at 155th (Cass county line)
LEFT at Prospect Ave

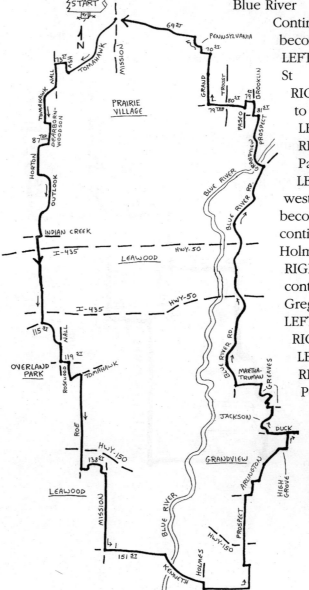

RIGHT on Arlington
RIGHT on High Grove
LEFT at Gradview
RIGHT at Duck Rd to Oden's Restaurant
Return east on Duck Rd
RIGHT on Jackson
LEFT at Greaves Rd
RIGHT at Merritt
LEFT on Martha Truman Rd
RIGHT on Blue River Rd.
LEFT on Grandview Rd. across Blue River
Continue across 85th becoming Prospect
LEFT at top of hill 81st St
RIGHT at Brooklyn to top of short hill
LEFT on 80th St
RIGHT on The Paseo
LEFT on 80th and west across Troost becoming 79th Terr. continuing across Holmes
RIGHT on Grand and continue north across Gregory
LEFT at 70th Terrace
RIGHT at Brookside
LEFT on 70th
RIGHT on Pennsylvania
LEFT at 69th St. and west across Ward Pkwy, State Line, Belinder, into Prairie Village

PRAIRIE VILLAGE TO OLATHE

Starting Point: Waid's Restaurant, Tomahawk & Mission, Prairie Village
Distance: 40+ miles
Degree of Difficulty: easy
Terrain: gently rolling
Things To See: a very popular KCBC ride on Saturday morning; breakfast stop at Waid's in Olathe

Cycle from Waid's southwest on Tomahawk Rd
RIGHT on Ash
LEFT at 73rd St
LEFT at Nall across 75th St
RIGHT on Tomahawk
LEFT on Dearborn across 79th and up a hill
Becomes Woodson at 83rd St
RIGHT at 87th Terrace
LEFT on Horton across 91st (with extreme caution)
Stay left on Outlook across 95th becomes Horton across 103rd

RIGHT at Indian Creek Drive
LEFT at Lamar and continue south across College
RIGHT on 115th across Metcalf (the light seems to change once daily)
LEFT on Lowell
RIGHT at 117th
LEFT at Hemlock across 119th th (caution)
RIGHT on 120th
LEFT on Mackey
RIGHT at 120th Terrace
LEFT at Antioch
RIGHT on 141st entrance to Nottingham South

LEFT on Switzer
RIGHT at 143rd west to Mur-Len and Mid-American Nazarene College
Becomes Sheridan which continues under I-35
LEFT at Ridgeview
RIGHT on Dennis Ave across Hwy 7 (Harrison) to Waid's at 912 S. Chestnut
Return the same route

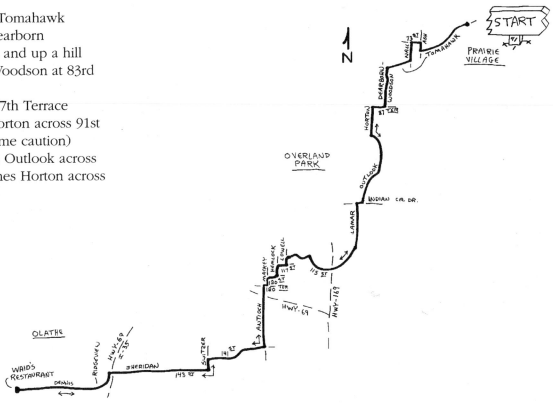

37

PRAIRIE VILLAGE TO DESOTO

Starting Point: Waid's Restaurant, Tomahawk & Mission, Prairie Village

Distance: 50 miles

Degree of Difficulty: moderately tough, especially the return

Terrain: moderately hilly

Things To See: new development along Blackfish and Midland, DeSoto, and Maria's Restaurant. This is a popular organized ride on Saturday mornings. The route is new to avoid the heavy traffic on 87th Pkwy and 83rd.

Cycle southwest on Tomahawk from Waid's Restaurant
RIGHT at 71st
RIGHT at Antioch
LEFT on 69th
RIGHT on Frontage Rd on east side of I-35
LEFT on 67th
LEFT at Farley which looks like a country lane
RIGHT at 69th
LEFT on Switzer
RIGHT on Edgewood

RIGHT at 75th
Continue west until it become Blackfish and then Midland
RIGHT at Renner
LEFT at Johnson Drive
LEFT on Clare Rd
RIGHT on 71st
LEFT at Mize
RIGHT at 83rd into DeSoto
Return the same way.

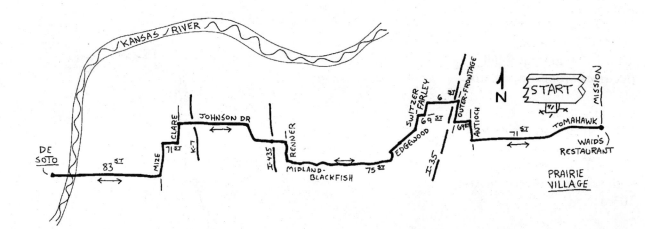

LOG CABIN RIDE

Starting Point: Waid's Restaurant, Tomahawk & Mission, Prairie Village
Distance: 26 miles
Degree of Difficulty: intermediate
Terrain: moderately hilly
Things To See: eat at The Log Cabin restaurant

Cycle east from Waid's Restaurant on 69th
RIGHT on Pennsylvania
LEFT at 70th across Wornall with care
RIGHT at Brookside Blvd
LEFT on 70th Terr
RIGHT on Cherry
LEFT at Gregory into Swope Park
RIGHT at T (Oldham Rd)
LEFT on 79th St for a "hill from hell"

RIGHT on James A Reed Rd
RIGHT at Greenwood where Mervin Jr. High is located
LEFT at Skiles
RIGHT on 107th St
RIGHT on Hillcrest
LEFT into Sleepy Hollow Apts at bottom of hill
LEFT at the T in the Apartment complex
RIGHT at Hickman Mills Rd to The Log Cabin Restaurant
Return north on Hickman Mills Rd
LEFT at a busy intersection of Bannister Rd and Hickman Mills Rd
Cycle west on shoulder
RIGHT and west on 95th St access road

RIGHT on Grandview Rd at top of hill
Continue north across Big Blue River to 85th where grandview becomes Prospect
LEFT at top of hill 81st St
RIGHT at Brooklyn to top of short hill
LEFT on 80th St
RIGHT on The Paseo
LEFT on 80th and west across Troost becoming 79th Terr. continuing across Holmes
RIGHT on Grand and continue north across Gregory
LEFT at 70th Terrace
RIGHT at Brookside
LEFT on 70th
RIGHT on Pennsylvania
LEFT at 69th St. and west across Ward Pkwy and State Line into Prairie Village

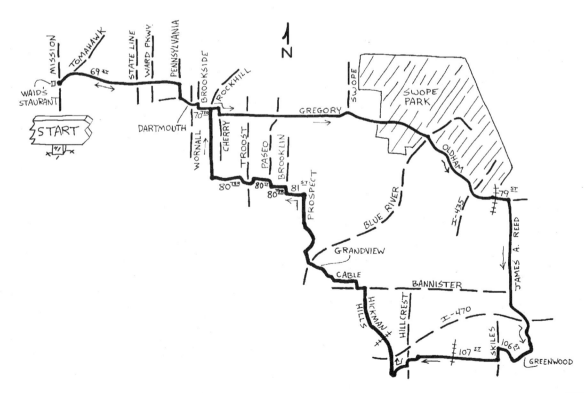

PRAIRIE VILLAGE TO LEE'S SUMMIT

Starting Point: Waid's Restaurant, Tomahawk & Mission, Prairie Village
Distance: 45 miles
Degree of Difficulty: intermediate
Terrain: moderately hills, with several challenging ones
Things To See: very unusual countryside along Little Blue, Thompson's Cafe in Lee's Summit with newspaper headlines on the wall.

This is one of the old favorites of the Saturday morning crowd led by Stuart Bitner.

Cycle east from Waid's Restaurant on 69th
RIGHT on Pennsylvania
LEFT at 70th across Wornall with care

RIGHT at Brookside Blvd
LEFT on 70th Terr
RIGHT on Cherry
LEFT at Gregory into Swope Park
RIGHT at T (Oldham Rd)
LEFT on 79th St for a "hill from hell"
Continue east on 79th
LEFT to 78th which winds into Woodson
RIGHT on 75th St
LEFT at Girl Scout Camp on Murkins Rd and across Noland Rd
Continue south on Little Blue Rd and the toughest hill of the ride (triple crank city)
LEFT on Gregory
RIGHT through Truman Med East
RIGHT on Lee's Summit Rd
LEFT at Strother
RIGHT at Hagan
LEFT on Jones Industrial Rd
RIGHT on Independence Ave

LEFT at Colbern Rd
RIGHT again at Independence Ave
RIGHT on Orchard
LEFT on Grand Ave
RIGHT at Douglas to Thompson's Cafe at Elm in downtown Lee's Summit
Return east on 3rd across Hwy 50
LEFT on Ward
RIGHT at Longview Rd
RIGHT at Longview Pkwy
LEFT on 109th
RIGHT on Elm
LEFT at 107th
RIGHT at James A Reed Rd
LEFT on 79th
RIGHT on Oldham Rd
LEFT at Gregory
RIGHT at Elmwood
LEFT on Mall Dr through main gate of Swope Park
Continue west on Meyer Blvd across Ward Pkwy at Meyer Circle
Continue west on Tomahawk to Waids in Prairie Village

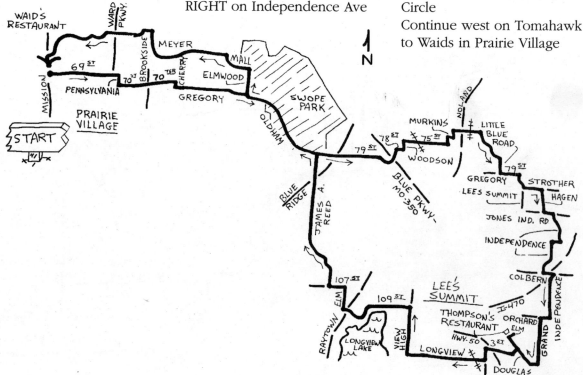

PRAIRIE VILLAGE TO GRANDVIEW

Starting Point: Waid's Restaurant, Tomahawk & Mission, Prairie Village
Distance: 35 miles (plus 10 mile loop of Longview Lake)
Degree of Difficulty: easy
Terrain: mostly flat and fast
Things To See: Blue River Rd the best cycling in the area. Eat at Oden's Restaurant in Grandview

This is probably the most popular of Saturday organized rides from Prairie Village. With south wind can really "fly" on ride home.

Cycle east from
Waid's Restaurant on
69th
RIGHT on
Pennsylvania
LEFT at 70th
across Wornall
with care
RIGHT at
Brookside
Blvd
LEFT on 70th Terr
RIGHT on Cherry
LEFT at Gregory into Swope Park
RIGHT at T (Oldham Rd)
RIGHT on Blue River Rd
LEFT on Blue Ridge Blvd
RIGHT at Prospect up short
steep hill across 129th
LEFT at Robinson Pike Rd
East on High Grove
LEFT on 10th
RIGHT at Main
LEFT at 13th
RIGHT on Duck to
Oden's Restaurant
Return east on Duck
Rd
RIGHT on Jackson

OPTION: return to Main StCycle east across
Hwy 71 on Highgrove up a long hill
LEFT at Sampson Rd
LEFT at Longview Rd
RIGHT on View High Rd
LEFT on Chipman Rd
LEFT at Raytown Rd back to Highgrove inter-section
Cycle west to Grandview and join return tour

LEFT at Greaves Rd
RIGHT at Merritt
LEFT on Martha Truman Rd
RIGHT on Blue River Rd.
LEFT on Grandview Rd. across Blue River
Continue across 85th becoming Prospect
LEFT at top of hill 81st St
RIGHT at Brooklyn to top of short hill
LEFT on 80th St
RIGHT on The Paseo
LEFT on 80th and west across
Troost becoming 79th Terr.
continuing across Holmes
RIGHT on Grand and con-
tinue north across
Gregory
LEFT at 70th Terrace
RIGHT at Brookside
LEFT on 70th St
RIGHT on Pennsylvania
LEFT at 69th St. and west across Ward Pkwy
and State Line
into Prairie
Village

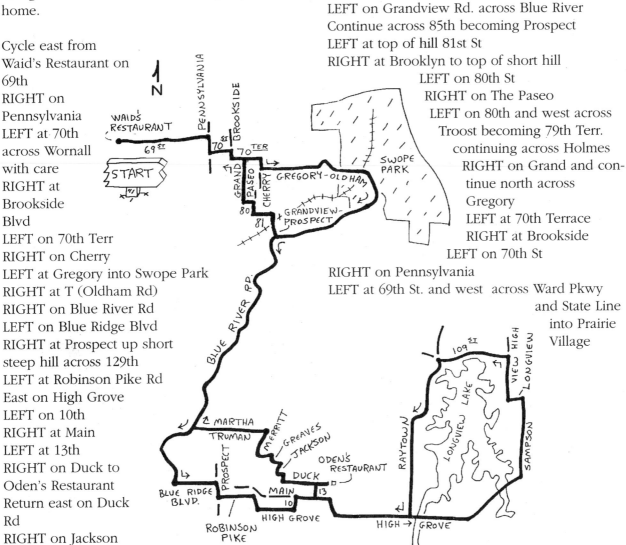

41

THE COLONEL'S RIDE

Starting Point: Loose Park tennis courts, 52nd Terrace & Summit
Distance: 14 miles
Degree of Difficulty: easy
Terrain: flat

This popular ride, named after the late Colonel Forrest G. Stith, meets at 2:00 PM every Sunday afternoon. It begins and ends at the Loose Park tennis courts and regroups at the Village Presbyterian Church, 67th 7 Mission Rd. A reverse route starts from Overland Park Primary School at Santa Fe & Robinson at 1:00 PM

This is required riding for newcomers to Kansas City or to cycling. If you want to meet other cyclists, there's likely to be 100-150 on a nice day.

Cycle west from Loose Park tennis courts on 52nd Terrace one block
LEFT on Belleview
RIGHT at 59th St
LEFT at Oakwood
RIGHT on Drury Lane thru the ford
LEFT on Mission Drive
RIGHT at 63rd St
LEFT one block on Indian Lane to the Village Presbyterian Church(regroup area)
LEFT on Mission Rd
RIGHT at 67th
LEFT at Delmar
RIGHT on 69th St
LEFT on Santa Fe
RIGHT at Marty
LEFT at 79th St
LEFT on Tomahawk
LEFT on Nall across 75th St
RIGHT at Tomahawk, across Mission Rd
RIGHT on 69th
LEFT on Valley Rd
LEFT at 63rd St on Summit north to Loose Park tennis courts

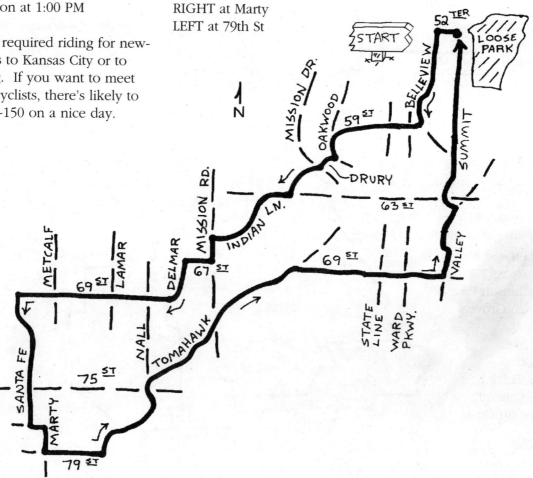

42

KANSAS CITY BICYCLE CLUB WELCOME RIDE

Starting Point: Loose Park tennis courts, 52nd Terrace & Summit
Distance: 20 miles
Degree of Difficulty: easy
Terrain: flat
Things To See: The Plaza, Downtown KC, Cliff Drive, Kansas City Museum

Cycle north on Summit from Loose Park tennis courts
RIGHT and quick left on 51st St
RIGHT at Ward Parkway
LEFT at Wornall bridge across Brush Creek
RIGHT on 46th Terr
LEFT on J.C. Nichols Pkwy
Continue north on Broadway
RIGHT at 26th
RIGHT at Pershing Rd
LEFT on Main St

RIGHT on Walnut
RIGHT at 19th St
LEFT at Holmes
RIGHT on 10th St
LEFT on Paseo
RIGHT at 9th St
LEFT at Woodland
RIGHT on Independence
LEFT on Maple to Cliff Drive
Cliff Drive exits at Gladstone Blvd
RIGHT at Gladstone Blvd to KC Museum
LEFT on Prospect
RIGHT on 9th St
LEFT at The Paseo
RIGHT at Linwood Blvd
LEFT on Gillham Plaza

LEFT on Gillham Rd
RIGHT at 48th St
LEFT at Rockhill Rd
RIGHT on Volker
LEFT on Oak
RIGHT at 51st to Loose Park tennis courts

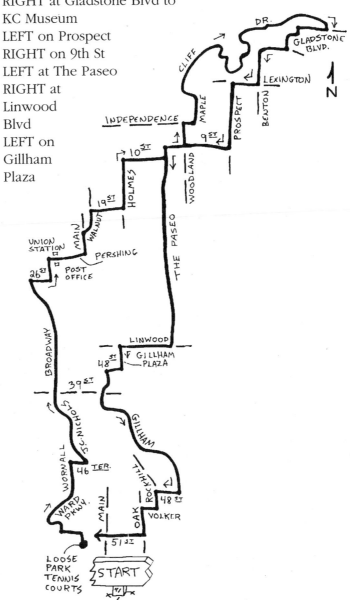

Starting Point: Bagel & Bagel, 63rd & Brookside
Distance: 24 miles
Degree of Difficulty: easy
Terrain: mostly flat

This ride was contributed by Mike Blaser. It was first introduced in November 1988, 6 months in advance of his annual Polski Day ride the first weekend in May. Those of us who know Mike Blaser can appreciate his sense of humor.

Cycle south on Brookside Blvd
LEFT on Gregory
RIGHT at The Paseo
LEFT at 85th
RIGHT on Prospect
LEFT on Blue River Rd
RIGHT at 67th
LEFT at Blue Ridge Cutoff
RIGHT on Blue Ridge Blvd
RIGHT on 63rd
LEFT at Raytown Rd
RIGHT at 59th
LEFT on Blue Ridge Blvd across I-70
RIGHT at fork and cycle east side of Mt. Washington Cemetery

LEFT at Winner Rd
LEFT on Ewing
LEFT on 17th to May's Grocery at 1654 Bristol
RIGHT at 17th
RIGHT at Topping
RIGHT on Belmont
LEFT on Cliff Drive
LEFT at Benton Blvd
RIGHT at 18th St
LEFT on Grand
LEFT on Gillham
Continue on Rockhill south
RIGHT at Volker
LEFT on Brookside Blvd back to starting point

75TH STREET BREWERY RIDE

Starting Point: 75th Street Brewery, 75th & Washington
Distance: 17 miles
Degree of Difficulty: not how far or how hard, but how fast
Terrain: mostly flat
Things To See: Every Tuesday night at 6:30 P.M. a group of 40-50 cyclists of varying degrees of ability looking forward to a "cool one" afterwards. One of the very best rides in all of Kansas City.

Cycle right on Washington
LEFT on 73rd
LEFT at Belinder
RIGHT at Somerset
LEFT on Outlook Drive
RIGHT on Indian Creek Dr.
LEFT at Lamar
LEFT at 115th St
LEFT on Nall
RIGHT on 99th St
LEFT at Delmar

RIGHT at 87th Place
LEFT on Catalina
RIGHT on Somerset
LEFT at Belinder
RIGHT at 73rd St
RIGHT on Washington to The Brewery

REALTOR'S RIDE I

WELCOME TO THE CUL-DE-SAC 500!

Starting Point: Prairie Star School, 143rd & Mission Road Distance: 15 miles not including anything extra through the subdivisions

Things To See: some of Johnson County's finest subdivisions. This ride can be started from any subdivision on the route. Be careful where you park.

Start at Prairie Star School, 143rd & Mission Road
Cycle north on Mission Rd
LEFT on 138th into Leawood Meadows
Exit Leawood Meadows with left on Roe and cycle west through Quail Crest
RIGHT(South) on Roe thru Worthington
North on Roe to 138th and weave east to Mission Road
RIGHT at Mission Road
RIGHT at 143rd
LEFT on Hemlock into Birchwood Place
RIGHT on Antioch
LEFT on 141st St thru Nottingham South
LEFT on Switzer
LEFT at 143rd
RIGHT at Antioch to 144th St and enter left the Villages of Kensington and Birchwood Place
LEFT (south) on Antioch to Wellington Park and its 3 subdivisons at 147th & 148th Sts.
RIGHT (south) on Antioch

LEFT at 159th
LEFT at Metcalf North to 158th St entrance to Willow Bend, Crescent Oaks, Sylvan Lake, and Creekside; lots of winding but stay east and you're okay.

Exit on Nall & south to 159th East to Mission Rd
North to Pavilions of Leawood at 148th & Mission Road
North on Mission Road & 143rd and the starting point.

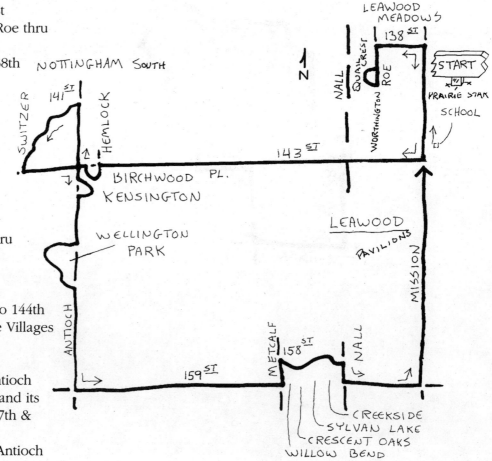

46

ROY'S PAOLA RIDE

Starting Point: Cedar Lake Park, south of
Olathe on Lone Elm Road
Distance: 40 miles
Degree of Difficulty: easy
Terrain: gently rolling
Things To See: Spring Hill, Hillsdale
Lake, Paola, and El Tapatio Restaurant

Cycle left on Lone Elm
LEFT on 143rd
LEFT on Hwy 56
RIGHT at 151st past Gardner Lake
LEFT at Gardner Road and cross
under I-35
LEFT at 199th
RIGHT on Webster after crossing
Hwy 169
South thru Spring Hill
RIGHT under Hwy 169
LEFT on Old Kansas City Road past Hillsdale at
255th (less traffic on 169 shoulder)
Cross Hwy 68 and take Hedge Lane into Paola
RIGHT at the High School to Baptist Drive and
El Tapatio Restaurant

Return the same way except when you are west-
bound on 199th after Spring Hill
RIGHT on Clare Rd
RIGHT on 175th
LEFT at Lone Elm to Cedar Creek Park

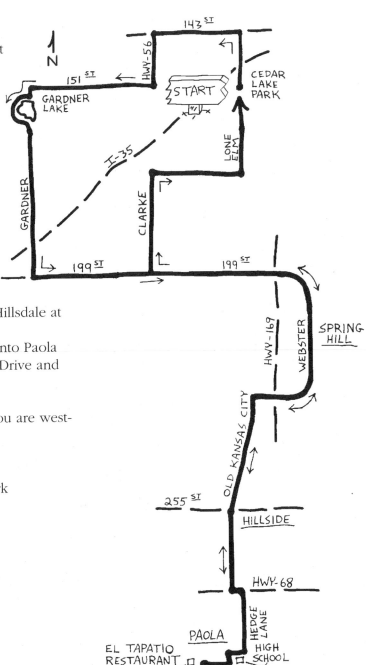

OLATHE TO LAWRENCE - A SOUTHERN ROUTE

Starting Point: Oregon Trail School, Dennis and K-7, Olathe

Distance: 50 miles

Degree of Difficulty: good workout

Terrain: rolling

Things To See: DeSoto, Eudora, and Lawrence; places to eat in Lawrence include Bluebird, Paradise, and Tin Pan Alley all on Massachusetts

Cycle west on Dennis (143rd St)
LEFT on Clare at Olathe Lake
RIGHT on 151st
RIGHT at Gardner Rd
LEFT at 127th
RIGHT on Waverly
LEFT on 115th
RIGHT at Kill Creek
LEFT (west) on Old K-10 through Eudora
RIGHT at industrial complex on gravel road
LEFT at 15h St

RIGHT on Massachusetts for eat and drink
Return south on Massachusetts
LEFT at 11th St
RIGHT at Haskell (D1055)
LEFT on D458
RIGHT on D1061
LEFT at D458
RIGHT at Dillie
LEFT on 151st past Gardner Lake
LEFT on Clare
RIGHT at Dennis to the starting point

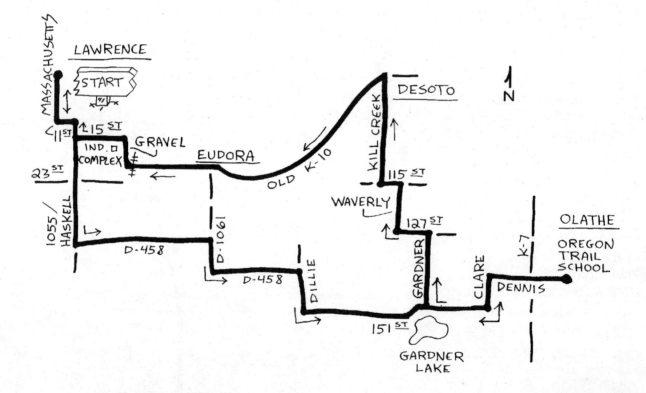

BALDWIN CITY ALMOST-METRIC

Starting Point: Oregon Trail School, 143rd & Parker, Olathe
Distance: 59 miles
Degree of Difficulty: good workout
Terrain: rolling
Things To See: Baldwin City, home of Baker University and the Maple Leaf Festival

Cycle west on Dennis (143rd)
LEFT Clare at Olathe Lake
RIGHT at 151st
RIGHT on Dillie
LEFT on 143rd (D458)
LEFT at D1061
RIGHT at D460
LEFT on D1055 into Baldwin City

LEFT at High
RIGHT where sign says 1900 E
Zoon
Return on US 56
Stay right after Edgerton Rd
LEFT at Four Corners
RIGHT at 175th
LEFT on Lone Elm to starting point

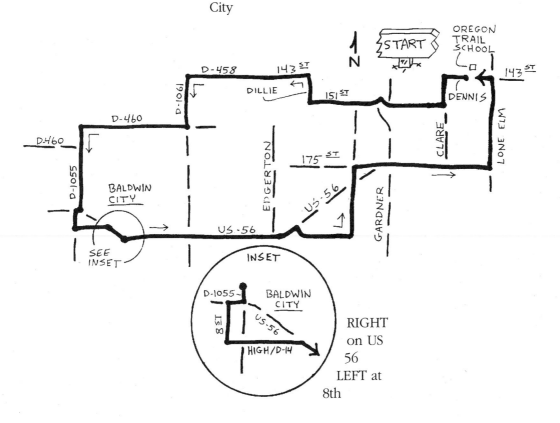

RIGHT on US 56
LEFT at 8th

OLATHE TO OTTAWA

Starting Point: Oregon Trail School, Dennis & Parker, Olathe
Distance: 80 miles
Degree of Difficulty: distance makes this ride difficult
Terrain: rolling
Things To See: towns of Olathe, Gardner, Edgerton, Wellsville, and Ottawa

Cycle west on Dennis
LEFT on Clare Rd at Olathe Lake
RIGHT at 151st
LEFT at Gardner Road North on west side of Gardner Lake
RIGHT on Main St (Hwy 56) past airport
LEFT on Rt 33 south thru Wellsville
RIGHT at Rt 68 to Ottawa
Return the same way.

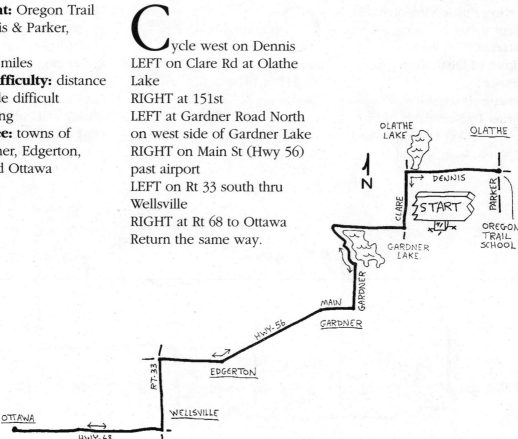

REALTOR'S RIDE II (OLATHE)

Starting Point: Santa Fe & Brougham Drive, Olathe
Distance: 15+ miles
Degree of Difficulty: easy
Terrain: flat
Things To See: Olathe subdivisions of Briarwood, Ashton, Havencroft, Brittany Meadows, and Stagecoach Meadows. Ride contributed by Dennis Jones of Prudential Summerson-Burrows.

Cycle south on Brougham Drive
LEFT on 139th
RIGHT at Brougham Drive
LEFT at 147th Terr
RIGHT on Blackbob to Heritage Park
LEFT through Park
RIGHT on Pflumm
RIGHT at 159th St

RIGHT at Ridgeview
RIGHT on Sheridan Bridge
LEFT on Lindenwood
RIGHT at 143rd St
LEFT at Summertree
RIGHT on 139th
LEFT on Broughman to starting point

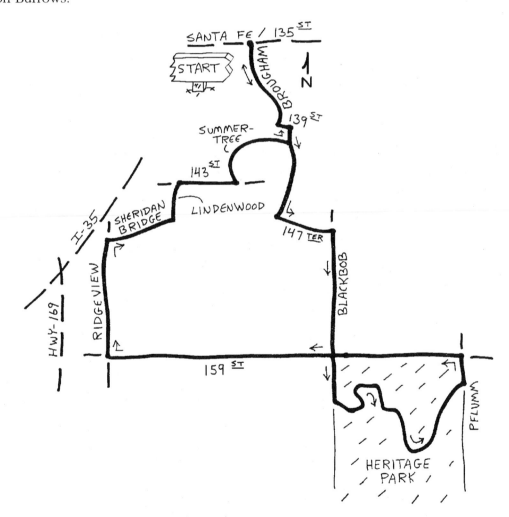

LAKE OLATHE RIDE

Starting Point: southside of Woodland & 119th
Degree of Difficulty: easy and friendly
Terrain: flat
Things To See: Lake Olathe via Ward Cliff Drive, and historic Olathe on Loula. Ride contributed by Dennis Jones.

Cycle south on Woodland Rd
RIGHT on Loula
LEFT at Parker
RIGHT at Dennis Ave
RIGHT on Ward Cliff Drive at Lake Olathe
RIGHT on Prairie Center Rd becomes Santa Fe when crossing K-7
LEFT at Kansas Ave
Continue north into Northgate
LEFT at Woodland to starting point

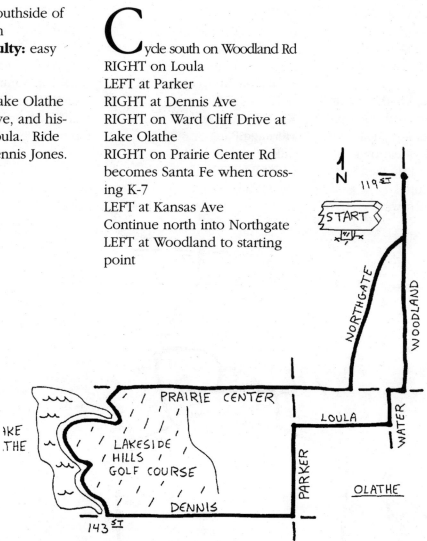

L.E.T.T.U.C.E. RIDE

Starting Point: Heritage Park Marina, 159th & Pflumm
Distance: 32 or 38 miles
Degree of Difficulty: comfortable
Terrain: rolling
Things To See: Another acronym with stands for Lower Exurbia Tour To Unveil Country Estates. This is an improved version of similar rides done by JCBC members.

Cycle west through Heritage Park from the Marina to Lackman exit
LEFT on Lackman
RIGHT on 191st
LEFT at Ridgeview
LEFT at 199th with Texaco 7-11 just past U.S. 69
LEFT on Mission

OPTION 6 mile extra loop - right on 159th, left at Kenneth, left at 143rd, and left on Antioch
Option shorter - left at 159th
LEFT at Antioch
RIGHT on 167th
LEFT on Switzer
RIGHT at 175th
RIGHT at Pflumm to Heritage Park Marina

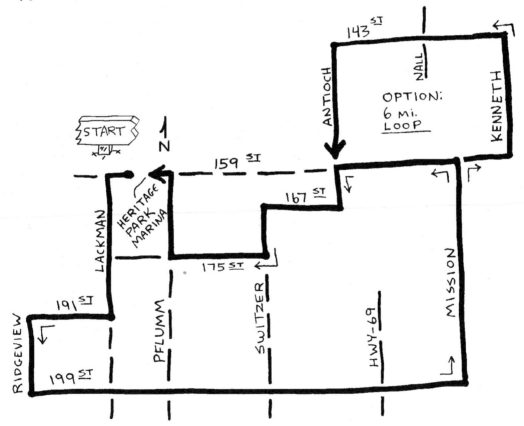

BUCYRUS OR BUST

Starting Point: Heritage Park marina, 159th & Pflumm
Degree of Difficulty: not really
Terrain: rolling
Things To See: southern Johnson County and northern Miami County. Another contribution by Mike Olin, JCBC

Cycle west from marina
LEFT on Lackman
RIGHT on 175th
LEFT at Clare
LEFT at 199th
RIGHT on Webster after K-7
LEFT on 223rd (Bucyrus Rd)
LEFT at Metcalf

RIGHT at 199th
LEFT on Mission Rd
LEFT on 159th
LEFT at Antioch
RIGHT at 167th
LEFT on Switzer
RIGHT on 175th
RIGHT at Pflumm to Heritage Park marina

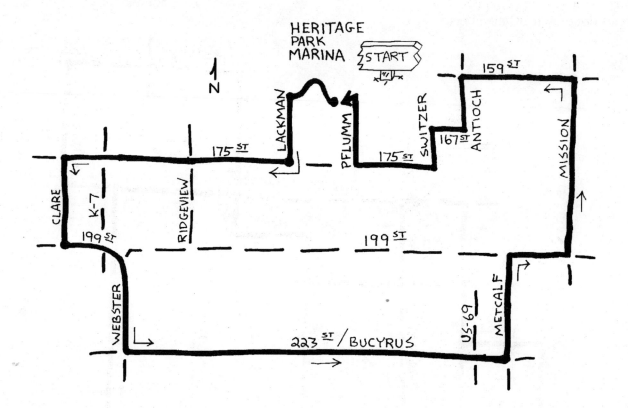

CAN'T GET LOST RIDE

Starting Point: Heritage Park, 159th & Pflumm
Distance: 37 miles
Degree of Difficulty: moderate
Terrain: rolling hills, east-west
Things To See: soon to be developed southern Johnson County. Not too busy route in the "country" by Dick Stephens. May be done clockwise or counter clockwise

Cycle from Heritage Park
LEFT on Lackman
RIGHT on 175th St
LEFT at Gardner Rd
LEFT at 199th
LEFT on Metcalf
LEFT on 179th
RIGHT at Switzer
LEFT at 175th
RIGHT on Pflumm to Heritage Park entrance

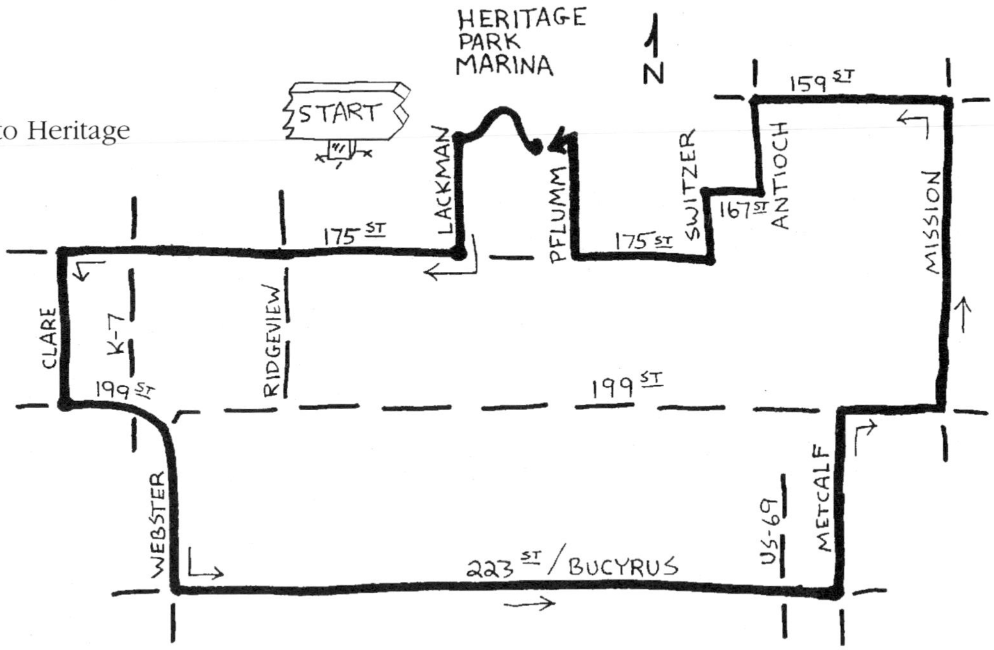

BILL'S BURRITO BLAST

Starting Point: Johnson County Community College, College Blvd and Quivira
Distance: 40 miles from JCCC; 25 miles from Olathe
Degree of Difficulty: not difficult unless windy; winds from south hasten the return trip
Terrain: Moderately hilly outward bound and rolling on the return usually with a tailwind
Things To See: Johnson County Community College campus, 11,000 students strong; downtowns of Olathe and Gardner; Olathe and Gardner Lakes; Trail Cafe in Gardner for burritos.

This organized ride, a creation of Bill Marsh over 12 years ago, has become a classic. Bill still leads the ride the second Sunday of each month. A second group of "late risers" join the group at the Johnson County Courthouse about 30 minutes after starting time at JCCC.

Cycle west from JCCC on College Blvd across I-35
LEFT on Renner Road
RIGHT at 119th across Ridgeview which becomes Northgate as it turns south
LEFT across 127th, then Kansas Ave. The Olathe courthouse and regroup area is on your right just as you cross Santa Fe
RIGHT on Park
LEFT on Pine
RIGHT at Elm
RIGHT at Dennis and west from Olathe
LEFT on Clare Road at Olathe Lake
RIGHT on 151st Street
Continue past Gardner Lake
LEFT (south) on Gardner Rd

LEFT on Main Street into downtown Gardner for burritos at Trail's Cafe
Return east on 175th with slight detour to the right opposite the Bank.
LEFT at Lone Elm
RIGHT at 143rd
LEFT after crossing the tracks and you at the Courthouse
Follow the same outbound route home from Olathe to JCCC.

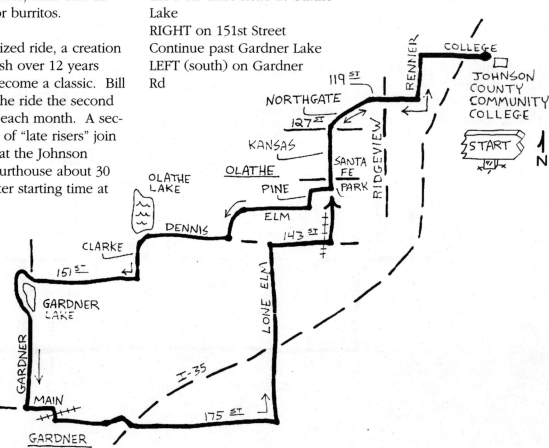

TAVERN RIDE

Starting Point: Johnny's Tavern, 119th & Glenwood
Distance: 23 miles
Degree of Difficulty: a good workout
Terrain: some hills but mostly rolling
Things To See: If it's a Glen Shepard ride, it's got to be good. Johnny's is a great place to play electronic trivial pursuit, says my daughter, Jennifer.

Cycle from Johnny's Tavern
RIGHT on Glenwood
LEFT on 123rd St
RIGHT at Lamar
LEFT at 127th St
RIGHT on Nall
LEFT on 143rd St
RIGHT at Mission Rd
RIGHT at 199th St
RIGHT on Metcalf
RIGHT on 119th St
RIGHT at Glenwood
RIGHT into Tavern parking lot.

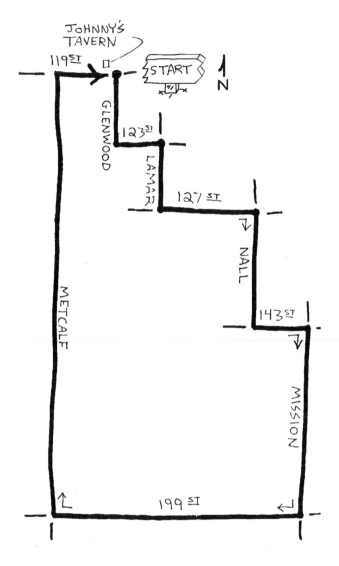

CORPORATE WOODS TO THE PLAZA

Starting Point: Corporate Woods North Park, 9401 Indian Creek Pkwy
Distance: 26.6 miles
Degree of Difficulty: easy
Terrain: flat to rolling
Things To See: Larry Stanfield of the Bungee Bike Club tells us this ride is good on Saturday and Sunday mornings. Sights to see are KC Sports Walk of Stars, Plaza fountains, Viet Nam Memorial, Loose Park

RIGHT on 47th St
LEFT on J.C. Nichols
Westport, N.E. corner for Corner Cafe - excellent for food
Return J.C. Nichols which dead ends at Board of Trade
LEFT at 48th
RIGHT at Main
RIGHT on 51st St
LEFT on 52nd (Summit)
RIGHT at 55th St
LEFT at Ward Parkway

RIGHT on Somerset (after 76th Pl)
LEFT on Lamar
RIGHT at College
RIGHT at Indian Creek Pkwy west of Antioch to North Park

Cycle from Corporate Woods North Park east on Indian Creek Pkwy
LEFT on Antioch
RIGHT at Santa Fe Drive
RIGHT at 79th St
LEFT on Tomahawk
LEFT counter clockwise around Meyer Circle fountain
Continue north on Ward Parkway
RIGHT at 55th St and straight on Sunset Dr (stay right at first fork) to Plaza
LEFT at Wornall

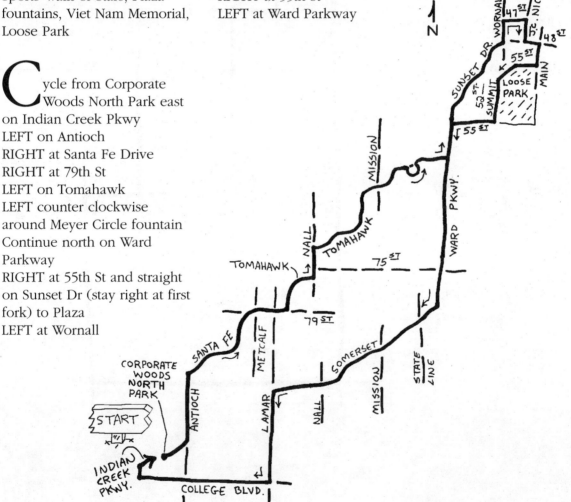

T.O.M.A.T.O. RIDE

Starting Point: Harmony Middle School, 143rd & Switzer
Degree of Difficulty: not very
Terrain: flat to rolling
Things To See: The name stands for Tour Of Meadows About To be Overdeveloped. This is a JCBC ride contributed by Mike Olin, who is obviously not in the real estate business.

Cycle west on 143rd
LEFT on Lindenwood before crossing I-35
RIGHT at Sheridan Bridge
LEFT at Ridgeview
LEFT on 175th
RIGHT on Switzer
LEFT at 179th
RIGHT at Metcalf

LEFT on 199th
LEFT on Mission
RIGHT at 159th
LEFT at Kenneth
LEFT on 143, after crossing Antioch, back to Switzer and the starting point.

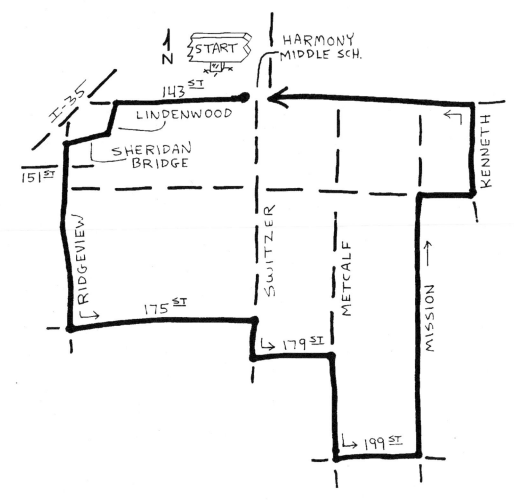

BLUE VALLEY POST OFFICE TO GARDNER

Starting Point: Blue Valley Post Office, 125th & Antioch
Distance: 38 miles
Degree of Difficulty: not too tough
Terrain: rolling hills
Things To See: Deanna Rose Petting Zoo, exotic animal farm at 159th & Switzer, Heritage Park, Johnson County airport, food in Gardner and Olathe. This ride compliments of Larry Stanfield, Bungee Bike Club.

Cycle from Post Office
RIGHT (north) on Antioch
LEFT on 119th
Turns left (south) on to Kansas City Rd
LEFT at Ridgeview
RIGHT at Dennis
LEFT on Dennis(Clare) at Lake Olathe
RIGHT on 151st St
LEFT at Moonlight
LEFT at 175th in Gardner; stop for food and drink
East on 175th through

LEFT on Pflumm at Heritage Park
RIGHT at 159th, Johnson County Airport
LEFT at Switzer
RIGHT on 143rd St
LEFT on Switzer
RIGHT at 141st at school
Cycle through Nottingham South
LEFT at Antioch back to Post Office at 125th & Antioch

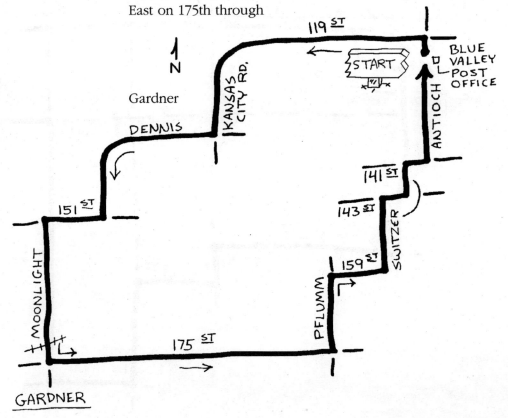

SHAWNEE MISSION PARK TO WYANDOTTE LAKE

Starting Point: Shawnee Mission Park, entrance on Renner
Distance: 50 miles
Degree of Difficulty: not for inexperienced riders
Terrain: hilly of Pflumm and very hilly around Wyandotte Lake Park
Things To See: a rare chance to see Wyandotte County; Wyandotte County Park is a discovery; food and drink at convenience stores only.

Cycle right (south) on Renner from Shawnee Mission Park
LEFT on 87th Pkwy.
LEFT at Pflumm
RIGHT at Johnson Drive
LEFT on Rosehill
RIGHT on 55th Street
LEFT at Halsey
Continue on 65th after crossing 47th
RIGHT on Holiday Drive
LEFT at 59th St.
RIGHT at Inland
LEFT on 55th Street
LEFT on Kansas Ave. in Turner and across the Kansas River Bridge with great caution.
Continue on K132 into Riverview
RIGHT on 86th St crossing State Ave

LEFT on Parallel
RIGHT at 91st into Wyandotte County Lake Park
Cycle the lake counter clockwise on an extremely hilly loop (6.5 miles)
Take a moment to enjoy the beauty and possibly the wildlife in Wyandotte County Park. It's a reminder how important our parks are. Return the same route.

SHAWNEE MISSION PARK TO LAWRENCE

Starting Point: Shawnee Mission Park, 87th Pkwy entrance
Distance: 55 miles
Degree of Difficulty: one of Johnson County's most popular rides
Terrain: mostly flat and fast except for two hills on return
Things To See: DeSoto and Eudora; Maria's restaurant in DeSoto hangout for cyclists; save some room for food and drink in Lawrence but keep in mind the return trip; it's tougher coming home than going.

Cycle west on 87th Pkwy from Shawnee Mision Park
Becomes 83rd when crossing K7
Continue through DeSoto and Eudora
OPTION, take Old K10 to Lawrence Industrial Park
RIGHT at Park over some gravel
LEFT on 15th
RIGHT on Masschusetts into the heart of Lawrence
Retrace your route back home

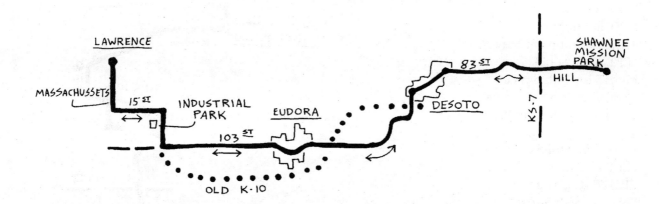

TCBK - THIS CAN'T BE KANSAS

Starting Point: Shawnee Mission Park entrance, 79th & Renner

Distance: 55 miles

Degree of Difficulty: you'll know you haven't been a couch potato today

Terrain: some hills

Things To See: DeSoto, Eudora, and Bonner Springs. This isn't Vermont or the Napa Valley. This ride contributed by Mike Olin of JCBC.

Cycle south on Renner
LEFT on 87th Pkwy which becomes 83rd after crossing K-7
RIGHT in DeSoto after pool and recreation area
LEFT at 82nd
RIGHT at Ottawa
LEFT on DeSoto N.W.
LEFT on Edgerton
RIGHT at 103rd
RIGHT across K-10
LEFT at D442 into Eudora

RIGHT on Main (D1061) at high school becomes L-1
RIGHT on K-32 past Linwood
RIGHT at L-26 joining L-2
RIGHT at L-32
LEFT on Loring into Bonner Springs (K-32)
RIGHT on K-7
LEFT at 55th
RIGHT at Barker which becomes Midland at Shawnee Mission Pkwy
RIGHT on Renner to park entrance

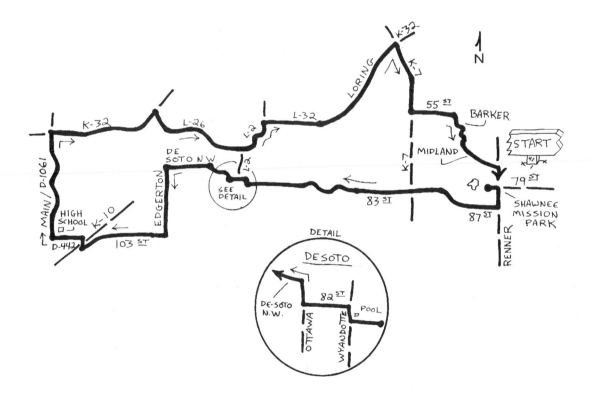

JOYCE'S TOUR OF SHAWNEE

Starting Point: Shawnee Mission NW School, 12701 W. 67th, Shawnee
Distance: 32 miles no option; 36.5 miles with option #2; 41.5 miles with option #1
Degree of Difficulty: a good workout
Terrain: moderately hilly
Things To See: Tomahawk & Shawnee Mission Parks, food & water Crouch's 55th & K-7, MacDonald's in Bonner Springs, Smiley's at K-7 & K-10, and Sonic at 63rd & Pflumm. This ride provided by Joyce Thompson.

Cycle west from school on 67th to second stop sign
LEFT on Midland
RIGHT(west) at Blackfish Pkwy
Continue west on Midland after crossing Lackman
Cross Shawnee Mission Pkwy
North on Barker
LEFT at Johnson Drive 2.5 miles to K-7

OPTION #1 to Bonner Springs
RIGHT on paved shoulder K-7
to Kansas Ave in Bonner Springs and "eats" at MacDonald's
Return on K-7 south
RIGHT at 55th
LEFT at Clare Rd
RIGHT on 63rd
LEFT on Mize Rd
LEFT at 71st
RIGHT at Gleason passing Monticello Church
LEFT on 83rd
RIGHT on K-7 to 95th
Exit at 95th, cross left over K-7
RIGHT at Frontage Rd (1 mile) with Smiley's on left
continue east on Frontage Rd
RIGHT at Woodland
  LEFT on 111th
  LEFT on Renner Rd to 79th

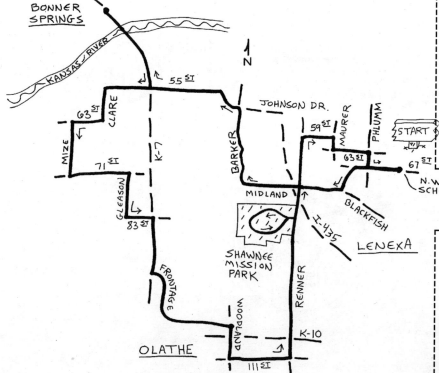

OPTION #2 circle Shawnee Mission Park (counter clock-wise 4.2 miles)
continue north on Renner
RIGHT at 59th Terrace
RIGHT at Maurer
LEFT on 63rd to Sonic on the right
RIGHT on Pflumm
LEFT at 67th St to Shawnee NW High School

LENEXA TO WOODLAND HILLS

Starting Point: Shopping Center on 87th Pkwy just east of Pflumm

Distance: 28 miles

Degree of Difficulty: short and easy

Terrain: one tough hill on Woodland coming back

Things To See: in the first book, this ride was featured as an underdeveloped woodsy ride. Not any more, 3 years later.

Cycle west on 87th Pkwy.
RIGHT on Pflumm
LEFT at 79th Street
RIGHT on Renner
LEFT on Holiday Drive with Lake Quivira to the right
RIGHT at stop sign in Holiday
LEFT at Woodland across 63rd St.
Continue south on Woodland with Monticello subdivision on right
LEFT on 111th across Renner Rd.
LEFT at College Blvd
LEFT at Pflumm to starting point

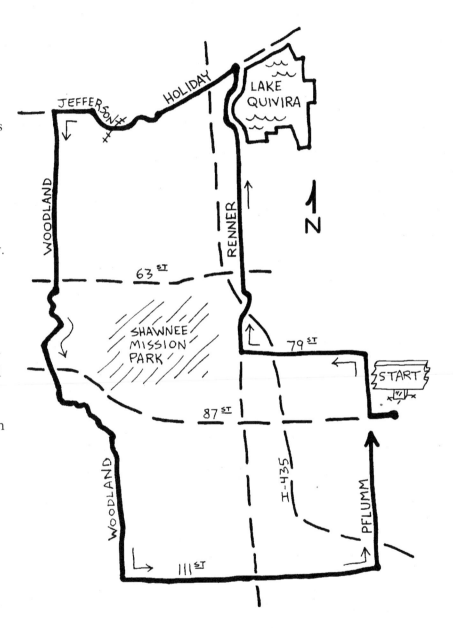

GARY RAND'S 5 HILL RIDE

Starting Point: Shopping Center, 87th Pkwy east of Pflumm
Distance: 35 miles
Degree of Difficulty: Ya gotta be kidding
Terrain: Very hilly
Things To See: One hill after another

Who ever said Kansas was flat? This is triple crank territory.

Cycle west on 87th Pkwy
RIGHT on Pflumm
LEFT at 79th St.

RIGHT at Renner Rd
LEFT on Midland which becomes Barker Rd. at 63rd St.
Continue on Barker past Johnson Drive
Continue northeast on Fred Smith Rd. through Holliday
East on Holiday Dr.
RIGHT at Quivira Lane
LEFT at 51st St
LEFT on Black Swan Dr

LEFT at Black Swan Lake and cycle clockwise to County Line - "Toto, I don't think we're in Kansas anymore"
RIGHT at 65th St
LEFT on County Line
RIGHT on Quivira
RIGHT at Johnson Drive
LEFT at Renner Rd
RIGHT on Midland Drive
LEFT on Ogg and enter Shawnee Mission Park
RIGHT on paved road counter clockwise around lake
Exit the Park on the east side at 79th St
RIGHT at Pflumm
LEFT at 87th Pkwy to start

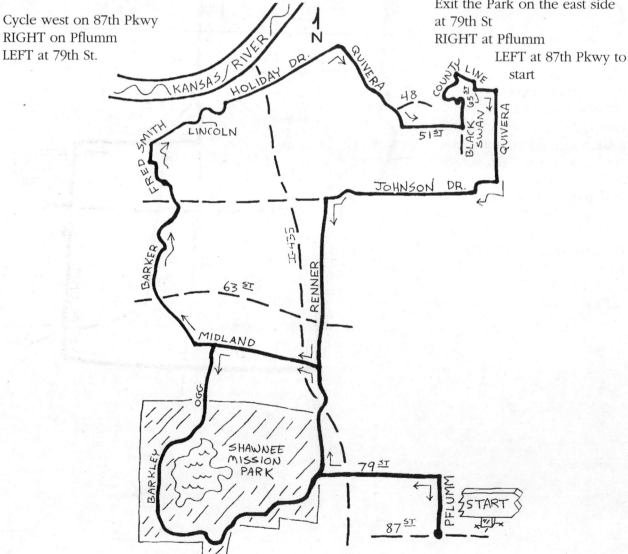

LENEXA TO KANSAS CITY MUSEUM

Starting Point: Shopping Center, 87th Pkwy, east of Pflumm
Distance: 42 miles
Degree of Difficulty: no problem
Terrain: mostly flat
Things To See: Downtown Kansas City, a variety of ethnic neighborhoods, Kansas City Museum, the River Market area, and parts of Kansas City, Kansas including Strawberry Hill

This is occasionally an organized ride on a Sunday morning, which, by the way, is the best time to do it. There's an option on the return called Escape From The Northeast.

Cycle east on 87th Pkwy
LEFT on Quivira
RIGHT at 79th St
LEFT at Goddard
RIGHT on Edgewood
LEFT on Switzer
RIGHT at 69th Terr.
LEFT at Farley
RIGHT on 67th St
LEFT on Carter
RIGHT at Merriam Dr which feeds in Southwest Blvd
LEFT at Grand
RIGHT on 19th St
LEFT on McGee
RIGHT at 8th St
LEFT at Flora
RIGHT on Admiral Blvd
LEFT on Woodland
RIGHT at Independence Ave
LEFT at Benton
RIGHT on Walrond

RIGHT on Gladstone Blvd

On return either use same as outbound or Escape Via River Market as follows:

West on Independence Ave
RIGHT on Cherry
LEFT at 3rd St
LEFT at Broadway
RIGHT on Woodswether Rd cross on abandoned bridge under Lewis & Clark
Continue on Minnesota Ave
LEFT on 5th
RIGHT on Splitlog
LEFT at 6th Ave
LEFT at 7th St
RIGHT on Central Ave
LEFT on Mill
RIGHT at Argentine Blvd
LEFT at 12th across Kansas River

RIGHT on Metropolitan Ave which turns southward after crossing 63rd St
Continue south on 65th at Oak Grove Rd
LEFT and continue south on Halsey
RIGHT on 55th
LEFT at Pflumm
LEFT at 87th Pkwy to start

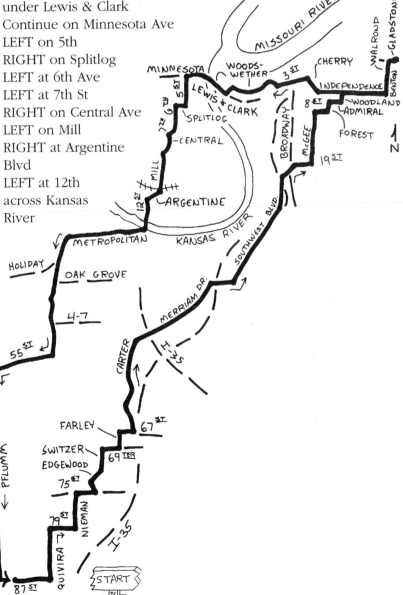

LENEXA TO MAXINE'S FINE FOODS

Starting Point: Shopping Center, 87th Pkwy, east of Pflumm
Distance: 35 miles
Degree of Difficulty: A "breeze"
Terrain: mostly flat
Things To See: Prairie Village, Mission Hills, The Plaza, and Maxine's (sounds like Maxim's)

This is a delightful organized ride on Sunday mornings. Good food and good company.
Cycle east on 87th Pkwy
LEFT on Quivira
RIGHT at 79th St
LEFT at Nieman Rd
RIGHT on 75th St
LEFT on Frontage Rd
RIGHT at 74th on south side of Shawnee Mission Hospital
LEFT at Antioch
RIGHT on 71st St

LEFT on Tomahawk
LEFT at State Line
RIGHT at Ward Parkway
LEFT on Wornall
LEFT on Pennsylvania
RIGHT at Westport Rd
LEFT at Broadway
RIGHT on 39th
LEFT on Main
RIGHT at Linwood
LEFT at Benton
Maxine's at 31st & Benton

Maxine's: home cooked breakfast with grits, hotcakes & great blues juke box

Return home the same way.

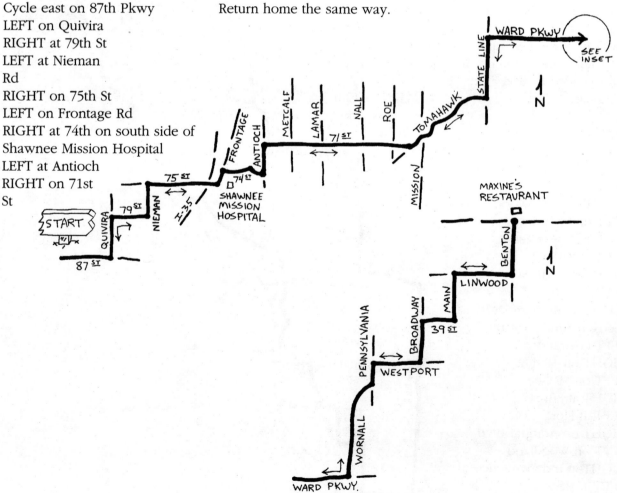

DON INBODY

also is an active member of Easy Riders. Don enjoys the companionship of senior riders and the bike trails.

JIM BURRUSS

is an active member of Easy Riders, a seniors bicycle group. Jim cycles for recreation and physical fitness. He promotes Easy Riders to get more "retired" folks interested in cycling.

Page

1. Realtor's Ride III (30)..73

2. Northland Show-N-GO # 1 (25)...........................74

3. Northland Show-N-Go # 2 (30)..........................75

4. Boardwalk To Platte City (35+)..........................76

5. Boardwalk To Trimble (40)................................77

6. Nostalgic Interurban Ride (30).......................... 78

7. Mr. Mac's Annual St. Pat's Ride (44).................. 79

8. Airport To Faucett (60)..................................... 80

9. Memorial Day Ride To Westport (26) 81

10. Antioch Mall To The Downtown Airport (18) 82

11. Northland To Cliff Drive (30)...........................83

12. Liberty To Platte City (50) 84

13. Liberty To Kearney (25) 85

14. Liberty To Plattsburg (53)................................ 86

15. Liberty To Watkins Mills (42)........................... 87

16. Smithville To Gower (58) 30............................88

17. Smithville To Plattsburg (55)............................89

18. Smithville To St. Joseph (80) 90

19. Excelsior Springs To Polo (60)..........................91

20. Plattsburg–Maysville Loop (60)........................92

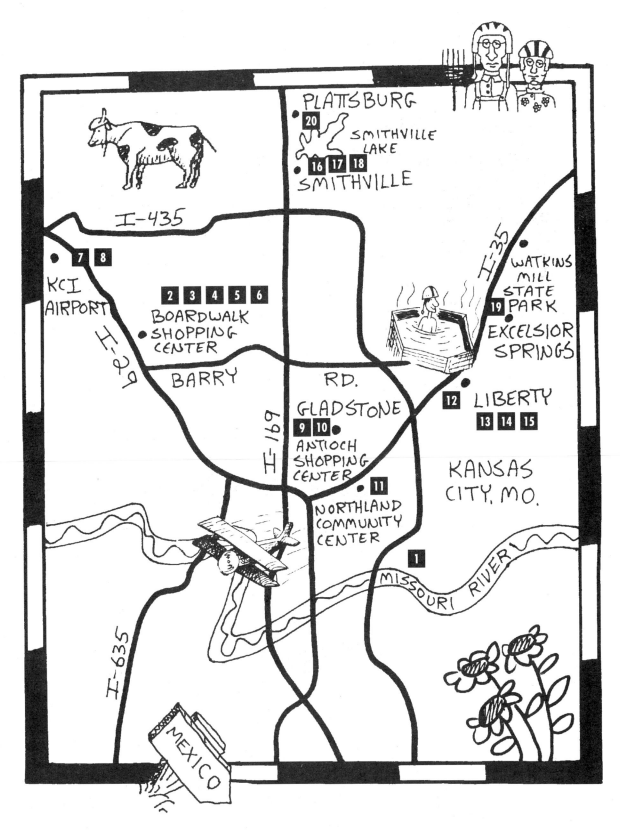

PLATTSBURG

20

SMITHVILLE
LAKE

16 17 18

SMITHVILLE

I-435

I-35

WATKINS
MILL
STATE
PARK

7 8

KCI
AIRPORT

I-29

2 3 4 5 6

BOARDWALK
SHOPPING
CENTER

BARRY

RD.

GLADSTONE

9 10

ANTIOCH
SHOPPING
CENTER

11

NORTHLAND
COMMUNITY
CENTER

19

EXCELSIOR
SPRINGS

12 LIBERTY

13 14 15

KANSAS
CITY, MO.

I-169

1

MISSOURI RIVER

I-635

MEXICO

LAURIE SCRUTCHFIELD

began cycling in 1988 in quest of fitness, comraderie, and adventure all rolled into one. Laurie gives back to cycling as much as she personally benefits as an active member of the Missouri Bike Federation and KCBC. Her efforts are directed toward seeing motorists and cyclists working together and "sharing the road." Her favortie areas to ride are in the Northland.

DAVE VAN WYCK

began cycling with the encouragement of friends in 1981. In the mid 1980's Dave discovered the Kansas City Bicycle Club which motivated him to ride longer distances, eventually experimenting with USCF racing and double centuries. Today he enjoys touring, club rides, and trying to keep pace with his wife, a competitve ultramarathon cyclist.

REALTOR'S RIDE III

Starting Point: it's a loop, so pick a point
Distance: 30 miles
Degree of Difficulty: moderate to challenging
Terrain: mixture of flats, rolling hills, and challenging hills
Things To See: Weatherby, Riss, and Houston Lakes. Parkville and Missouri Bluffs plus ice cream en route. A terrifc way to see the many subdivisions in the Northland says Laurie Scrutchfield, Northland KCBC.

CYCLE north on Westside Drive
RIGHT on Pleasant Ford into Potomac
RIGHT at Wayland
LEFT at Hillside
RIGHT on sidewalk of Barry Rd
LEFT on Amity
RIGHT at Tiffany Springs Rd around front of Ramada Inn
RIGHT at Prairie View
LEFT on Congress to first T
LEFT on Belvidere (cross thru Texaco)
RIGHT at Prairie View
LEFT at 72nd
RIGHT on Cosby
LEFT on Park Plaza Drive
RIGHT at 70th
RIGHT at Overland
LEFT on 67th Terr.
RIGHT on Oregon
RIGHT at 67th St
LEFT at Overland
Continue south across Hwy 45, becomes Roanridge
Curves into 56th, becomes

Helena
LEFT on W. Platte Rd
RIGHT on Hwy 9 (River Rd) into Parkville
LEFT at Main
RIGHT at Mill exit Parkville on FF (past Bluffs)
RIGHT on Indian Hill Lane and gear for hill
RIGHT on Raintree Drive
RIGHT at Crooked Rd and long lcimb
LEFT at Mill back to Parkville
LEFT on Main
LEFT on Hwy 9
RIGHT at Lakeview Dr into Riss Lake
Continue on Riss Lake Drive north
RIGHT on 64th
LEFT at Cosby for ice cream & yogurt

RIGHT at St Clair becomes Caney Creek
RIGHT on Montrose
RIGHT jog on 72nd
LEFT at Maple
Continue west on 73rd into Lingley
RIGHT at T on Eastside Dr into Weatherby Lake
LEFT at 72nd Terr curving left over dam
RIGHT on Kerns into 76th
Follow lake shore back on Westside Drive

Starting Point: Boardwalk Shopping Center, east of I-29 on Barry Road
Distance: 25 miles
Degree of Difficulty: moderate
Terrain: mostly rolling with a few good climbs
Things To See: Historic downtown Parkville, Park College, English Landing Park, Houston Lake. David Van Wyck contributed this Thursday night Northland KCBC ride.

Cycle east from Boardwalk Square parking lot, heading north on Executive Hills Blvd
RIGHT on St. Clair
LEFT at Waukomis
RIGHT at 86th Terrace
RIGHT on Beaman
LEFT on Barry Rd
LEFT at Green Hills
LEFT at Tiffany Springs
LEFT on Sky View (this short section takes you over I-29 with Ramada on your right)
LEFT on Prairie View
LEFT at Congress
RIGHT at 79th Place
LEFT on Mace
RIGHT on Lingley Dr
RIGHT at Eastside Dr
LEFT at Blair Rd
LEFT on Cross Rd
RIGHT on Melody(Cross gradually veers into Melody and crosses Hwy 9 at stoplight)
Cycle through Parkville Heights Shopping Center staying to the left and in back
RIGHT at 63rd St
LEFT at Bell Rd

LEFT on Hamilton
RIGHT on Wst St
LEFT at FF
LEFT at Main St
If it's Saturday morning, try McKeon's for breakfast, or English Landing coffee, and there's a farmers market in the park.
RIGHT on Hwy 9 which has a good shoulder
LEFT on Platte Rd
RIGHT at Green Hills
RIGHT at 52nd St
LEFT on Northwood
RIGHT on 56th St
Cross under I-29 and follow the frontage road to the left
RIGHT at Lenox
RIGHT at Oakcrest
LEFT on Robinhood
RIGHT on 64th St
LEFT at Daggett
LEFT at 68th St which becomes Waukomis almost immediately
LEFT on Bryan
RIGHT on Linden

RIGHT at Overland
LEFT at 72nd and cross under I-29
LEFT on Maple
Cross Hwy 9 and Maple turns into NW 73rd St
RIGHT on Mace
RIGHT at 79th Pl
LEFT at Congress
RIGHT on Prairie View
RIGHT on Skyview across I-29
RIGHT at Tiffany Springs
RIGHT at Green hills
RIGHT on Barry Rd
RIGHT on Beaman
LEFT at 86th Terr
RIGHT at Waukomis
RIGHT on St. Clair
LEFT on Executive Hills Blvd and you're home

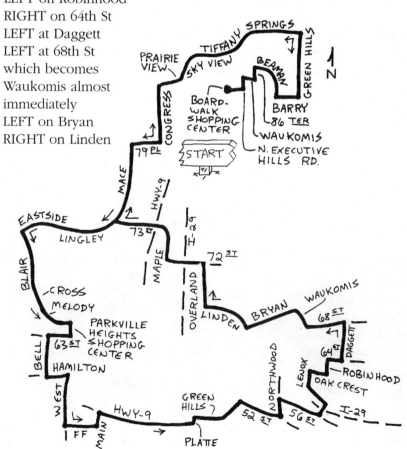

Starting Point: Boardwalk Shooping Center under the flag, Barry Rd east of I-29
Distance: 30 miles
Degree of Difficulty: easy
Terrain: gently rolling hills, with long flat stretch on Interurban
Things To See: follows the route of the old Interurban trolley line

Cycle from Board Walk Square parking lot east
RIGHT (north) on Executive Hills Blvd
RIGHT on St. Clair
LEFT at Waukomis
RIGHT at 86th Terrace
RIGHT on Beaman
LEFT on Barry Rd
LEFT at Green Hills
LEFT at Tiffany Springs
LEFT on Sky View
LEFT on 128th
RIGHT at Interurban
LEFT at HH
LEFT on Bethel
LEFT on Prairie View
RIGHT at Mexico City Ave
LEFT at Bern
LEFT on Hwy 291 for short distance (caution)
Look for row of conifers in ditch on right. Take faint path leading to frontage road (Prairie View)
LEFT at Ramada Inn across I-29

RIGHT on Tiffany Springs
RIGHT on Green Hills
RIGHT at Barry Rd
RIGHT at Beaman
LEFT on 86th Terrace
RIGHT on Waukomis
RIGHT at St. Clair
LEFT at Executive Hills Blvd and back home

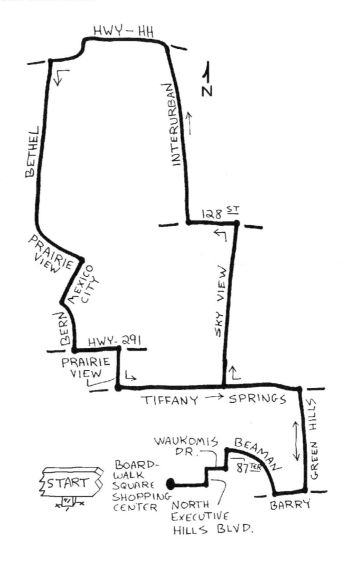

BOARDWALK TO PLATTE CITY

Starting Point: Boardwalk Shopping Center, Barry Rd east of I-29

Distance: 35+ miles

Degree of Difficulty: comfortable

Terrain: mostly flat with a few hills around Platte City

Things To See: Eat at Fannie's Restaurant in Platte City

Cycle east and north of shopping center
RIGHT at Hwy T
LEFT at Green Hills
LEFT on Tiffany Springs Rd
RIGHT on Skyview
LEFT at 128th
RIGHT on Winan
LEFT on 132nd
RIGHT at Roanridge
RIGHT at Bethel
LEFT on Hwy HH to Fannie's at 4th & Main in Platte City
RETURN on Marshall south past Main
RIGHT at Outer Dr
LEFT at 136th
RIGHT on Mexico City Ave
LEFT on Bern St
LEFT at MO 291
RIGHT immediately past "Welcome to KC" sign on Prairie View
LEFT at Tiffany Springs
RIGHT on Green Hills
RIGHT on Hwy T
LEFT into Boardwalk

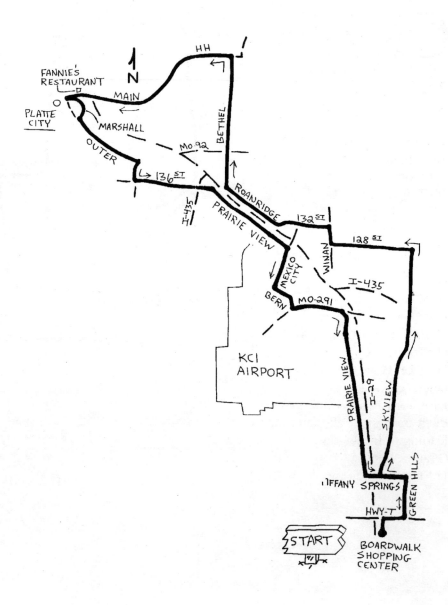

BOARDWALK TO TRIMBLE

Starting Point: Boardwalk
Shopping Center, Barry Rd east
of I-29
Distance: 40 miles
Degree of Difficulty: good
ride
Terrain: moderately hilly
Things To See: food and drink
at Smithville Lake. Good view
of the lake from the dam.

Cycle north and east from
the shopping center
RIGHT on Hwy T
LEFT on Green Hills
LEFT at Tiffany Springs
RIGHT at Skyview
LEFT on 128th
RIGHT on Interurban
RIGHT at MO 92
LEFT at Hwy B
RIGHT on Hwy KK
RIGHT on Spur 69
LEFT at Hwy F
LEFT at Oak into Trimble
Return east on Oak
RIGHT on Hwy F
LEFT on Hwy DD across dam
RIGHT at Main St west across
Hwy 169 past Bridge Rd
LEFT at 2nd Creek
RIGHT on MO 92
LEFT on Hwy C which mean-
ders southwest and becomes
Skyview
LEFT at Tiffany Springs
RIGHT at Green Hills
RIGHT on Hwy T
LEFT into Boardwalk Shopping
Center

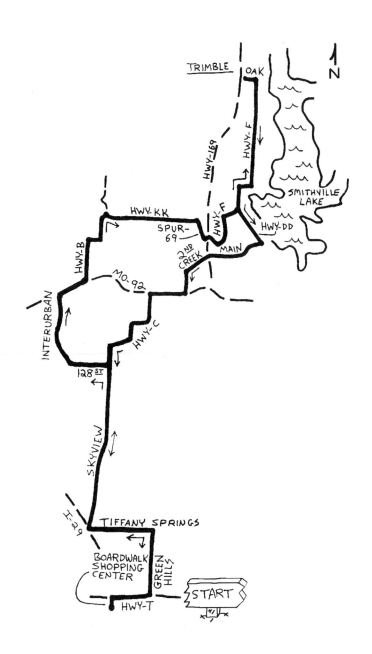

NOSTALGIC INTERURBAN RIDE

Starting Point: Boardwalk Shopping Center, Barry Rd east of I-29
Distance: 30 miles+
Degree of Difficulty: easy
Terrain: flat to rolling
Things To See: same route as traversed by the old interurban trolley. This ride compliments of Laurie Scrutchfield and her Northland group

Cycle east from Boardwalk and then head north
RIGHT on St. Clair
LEFT at Waukomis Dr
LEFT at 86th Terr
RIGHT on Beamon
LEFT on Barry Rd (on sidewalk if desired)
LEFT at Green Hills Rd
LEFT at T on 108th
RIGHT on Skyview across Hwy 291 becoming Hwy C
LEFT on Hwy 92, caution traffic
LEFT at Interurban, becomes Heady at Ferrelview
RIGHT at first chance with Kwik Shop on left
RIGHT on Cookingham
LEFT on Ambassador Dr thru Airworld Center
Straight at stop sign on Tiffany Springs Pkwy
AT World Span curve around proceeding east

LEFT at Skyview
RIGHT on 108th
RIGHT on Green Hills Rd
RIGHT at Barry Rd
RIGHT at Beaman, turns into 86th Terr
RIGHT at T on Waukomis
RIGHT on St. Clair
LEFT on Corner returning to Boardwalk.

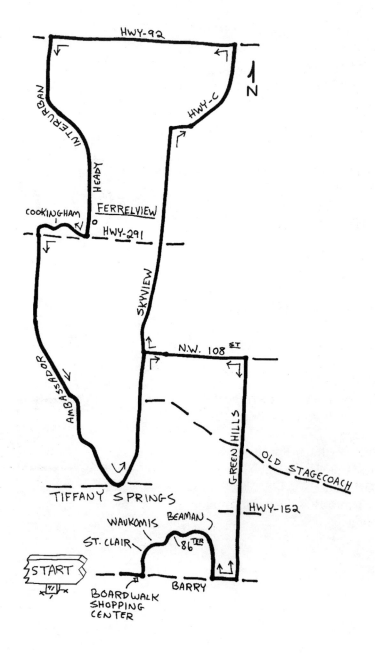

MR MAC'S ANNUAL ST PAT'S RIDE

Starting Point: Ramada Inn at KCI, I-29 North at Tiffany Springs exit
Distance: 44 miles
Degree of Difficulty: comfortable
Terrain: mostly flat with some rolling hills
Things To See: this 44 mile ride to Edgerton has been Mac McCallister's St. Pat's ride for several years. For food try Harmer's Cafe in Edgerton.

Cycle west from the Ramada Inn on Tiffany Springs Rd
RIGHT on Amity
RIGHT on 104th
LEFT at Prairie View
RIGHT at 112th across I-29
LEFT on Ambassador
RIGHT on Heady
LEFT on Congress
RIGHT at Hwy 92
LEFT at B
RIGHT on E
LEFT on B to Harmer's Cafe in Edgerton
Return south on B
RIGHT at E
LEFT at B
LEFT on Hwy 92
RIGHT on C across Hwy 291 becoming Skyview
RIGHT at Tiffany Springs Rd to Ramada Inn

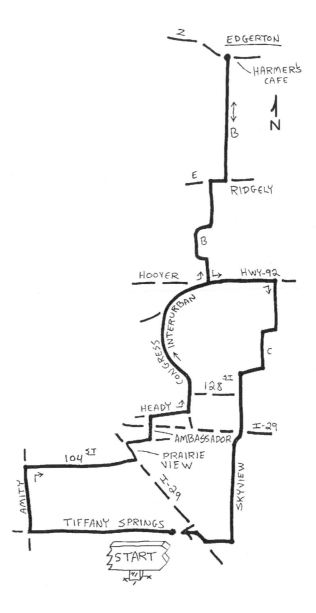

AIRPORT TO FAUCETT

Starting Point: Ramada Inn at I-29 & Tiffany Springs Rd
Distance: 60 miles
Degree of Difficulty: moderate
Terrain: mostly flat with rolling hills after New Market
Things To See: Tobacco farms at southern end of MO 371. Eat at Oliver's Restaurant in Faucett says Ken McFarland.

Cycle east across I-29
LEFT (north) on Skyview
LEFT on 128th
RIGHT at Winan
LEFT at 132nd
Stay right on Mexico City Ave
LEFT on Bethel across I-29
RIGHT at Prairie View
RIGHT at 136th before Broken Bridge Rd
LEFT on Hwy J which parallels I-29 on the west
RIGHT on MO 273
LEFT at MO 371 north past New Market
Eat at Oliver's Restaurant, I-29 & H
RIGHT at Hwy Y(south) to Dearborn
RIGHT at Hwy H across I-29
LEFT on MO 371
RIGHT on Spur 92
LEFT at Hwy J
LEFT at MO 92
RIGHT on Bethel
LEFT on 132nd following I-29 on the east side
RIGHT at Winan
LEFT at 128th
RIGHT on Skyview to starting point

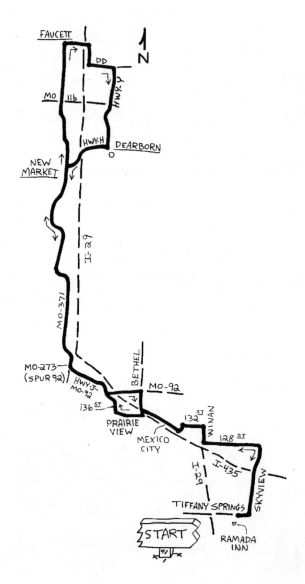

MEMORIAL DAY RIDE TO WESTPORT

Starting Point: Antioch Mall, corner of Vivion & Chouteau Tfwy
Distance: 26 miles
Degree of Difficulty: moderate
Terrain: always a climb away from the river
Things To See: War Memorial, Viet Nam Memorial, Liberty Memorial, Fireman's Memorial, and breakfast at Bagel Works or Bagel & Bagel in Westport. Credit for this ride goes to Jim Pfeffer and Art Loepp.

Cycle from Antioch Mall east on 53rd St
LEFT on 52nd Terrace
RIGHT at Jackson
RIGHT at Vivion
LEFT on Norton
RIGHT on 46th St
LEFT at Chouteau Tfwy
1/2 RIGHT at Cleveland
RIGHT on Parvin
LEFT on Winn
LEFT at Antioch
which turns into Bell then Walker
RIGHT at Armour or 210
RIGHT on Ozark
LEFT on 24th Ave
LEFT at Howell (2nd left at intersection)
War Memorial in the median between Iron and Howell at 23rd Ave

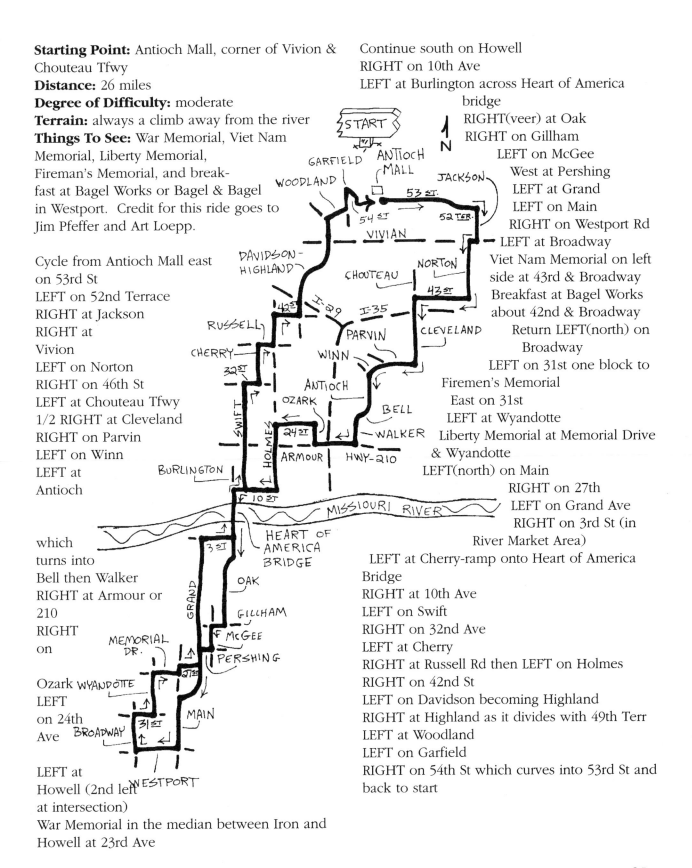

Continue south on Howell
RIGHT on 10th Ave
LEFT at Burlington across Heart of America bridge
RIGHT(veer) at Oak
RIGHT on Gillham
LEFT on McGee
West at Pershing
LEFT at Grand
LEFT on Main
RIGHT on Westport Rd
LEFT at Broadway
Viet Nam Memorial on left side at 43rd & Broadway
Breakfast at Bagel Works about 42nd & Broadway
Return LEFT(north) on Broadway
LEFT on 31st one block to Firemen's Memorial
East on 31st
LEFT at Wyandotte
Liberty Memorial at Memorial Drive & Wyandotte
LEFT(north) on Main
RIGHT on 27th
LEFT on Grand Ave
RIGHT on 3rd St (in River Market Area)
LEFT at Cherry-ramp onto Heart of America Bridge
RIGHT at 10th Ave
LEFT on Swift
RIGHT on 32nd Ave
LEFT at Cherry
RIGHT at Russell Rd then LEFT on Holmes
RIGHT on 42nd St
LEFT on Davidson becoming Highland
RIGHT at Highland as it divides with 49th Terr
LEFT at Woodland
LEFT on Garfield
RIGHT on 54th St which curves into 53rd St and back to start

81

ANTIOCH MALL TO THE DOWNTOWN AIRPORT

Starting Point: Antioch Shopping Center, 53rd & Antioch

Distance: 18 miles plus 3.9 extra miles for each loop of the airport

Degree of Difficulty: fast and easy

Terrain: mostly flat except for uphill on Cherry

Things To See: eat at Chappell's in NKC afterwards. Show your stuff around the airiport.

Cycle west on 53rd St which angles into 54th
LEFT on Garfield
RIGHT at 49th
LEFT at Highland crossing Vivion and I-29
RIGHT on 42nd St
LEFT on Holmes downhill, becomes Howell at 32nd
RIGHT at 16th
LEFT at Atlantic across railroad tracks

RIGHT on Harlem which becomes Lou Holland Dr and Richards Road, both circling the airport
Return on Harlem
LEFT at Atlantic
RIGHT at 10th Ave
LEFT on Swift
RIGHT on 32nd
LEFT at Cherry
RIGHT at Terrace
LEFT on Holmes
RIGHT on 42nd
LEFT at Highland
RIGHT at 49th
LEFT on Garfield
RIGHT on 54th, then 53rd to Antioch Shopping center

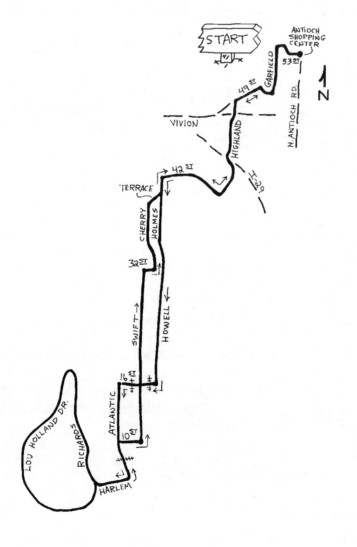

NORTHLAND TO CLIFF DRIVE

Starting Point: Northland Community Center, Antioch & Parvin Rd
Distance: 30 miles
Degree of Difficulty: easy
Terrain: flat, only hill on Holmes Rd return
Things To See: scenic Cliff Drive. Cycle at low traffic times on Heart of America Bridge. It's dangerous at best!

RIGHT on Belmont
RIGHT on Gladstone Blvd
RIGHT at Cliff Drive
LEFT at Missouri
RIGHT on Highland
RIGHT on Independence Ave
RIGHT at Charlotte
LEFT at 3rd (also Industrial)
RIGHT on Heart of America Bridge

RIGHT on 14th
LEFT at Swift
RIGHT at 32nd
LEFT on Cherry
RIGHT on Terrace
RIGHT on Russell which becomes Parvin Rd at I-35
Take Parvin Rd east to Northland Community Center

Cycle west on Parvin Rd which becomes 42nd St
LEFT on Holmes
RIGHT at 32nd St
LEFT at Burlington, across Heart of America Bridge (cycle with traffic, on the right, and with caution)
RIGHT on Admiral
RIGHT on Grand
RIGHT at 3rd St which becomes Industrial, crosses Guinotte, then becomes Lydia
LEFT at Front St
LEFT on River Front Rd
RIGHT on Chouteau
LEFT at Stilwell
RIGHT at Topping
LEFT at Equitable
LEFT on Universal
RIGHT on Executive
RIGHT at Universal
U-TURN at Equitable back to Universal
LEFT on Front
RIGHT on Century
]RIGHT at Hawthorn
LEFT at Chouteau

LIBERTY TO PLATTE CITY

Starting Point: Liberty Court House parking lot, Mill St in Liberty
Distance: 50 miles
Degree of Difficulty: challenging
Terrain: moderately hilly
Things To See: This ride is a combination of several others. The roads are constantly changing, so be patient and understanding with us. It's an interesting combination of urban and rural (more and less). Food at Fannie's in Platte City

Cycle north on Gallatin
LEFT on Nashua across I-35
LEFT at 96th St (NN) and across I-435
RIGHT at Brighton
LEFT on Staley Rd
LEFT on Woodland
RIGHT at 106th
RIGHT at N. Oak Tfwy
LEFT on 108th
RIGHT on Skyview
LEFT at 128th
RIGHT at Interurban
LEFT on HH into Platte City for food at Fannie's
Return the same route

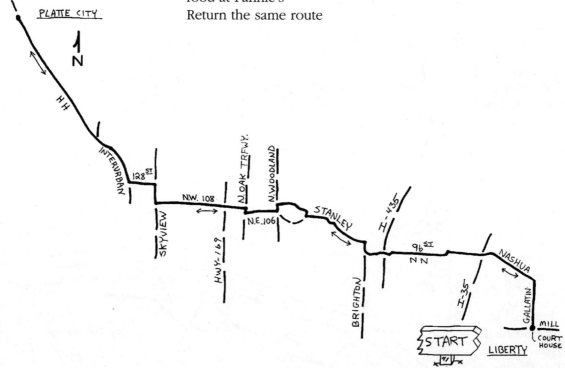

84

LIBERTY TO KEARNEY

Starting Point: William Jewell campus in Liberty
Distance: 25 miles
Degree of Difficulty: easy
Terrain: mostly flat
Things To See: William Jewell's campus in Liberty, Clem's Restaurant in Kearney

Cycle east on Hwy H
LEFT on Hwy B which becomes MO 33
RIGHT at Washington St to Clem's in Kearney
West on Washington
RIGHT on MO 33
LEFT at 162nd St
LEFT at Lightburne south into MO 33
RIGHT on Hwy H to the campus

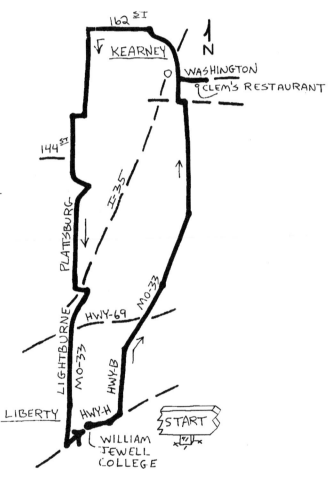

LIBERTY TO PLATTSBURG

Starting Point: William Jewell campus in Liberty
Distance: 53 miles
Degree of Difficulty: challenging
Terrain: moderately hilly
Things To See: this ride goes due north passing Smithville Lake on the east side. Bert & Ernie's is the place to eat in Plattsburg but it's closed on Sunday.

Cycle north on Lightburne (MO 33)
LEFT on 162nd
RIGHT at Old Plattsburg Rd
RIGHT at Hwy C
LEFT on Broadway to Bert & Ernie's in Plattsburg
Return on Broadway
RIGHT at Hwy C
LEFT at MO 92
RIGHT on Hwy A
LEFT on 144th (Arthur)
RIGHT at Lightburne Rd to William Jewell

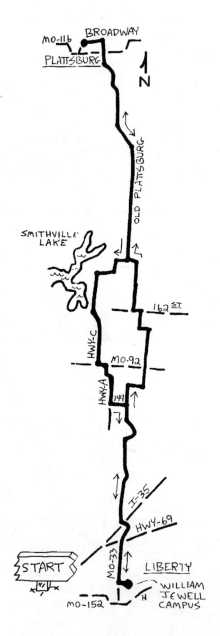

LIBERTY TO WATKINS MILLS

Starting Point: William Jewell campus in Liberty

Distance: 42 miles

Degree of Difficulty: navigation might be the only problem

Terrain: mostly flat

Things To See: the woolen mill and other sights in Watkins Mill State Park, Jesse James farm, and Clem's Restaurant in Kearney.

Cycle east on Hwy H
LEFT on Hwy B
RIGHT at Neth
LEFT at Stockdale
RIGHT on Hwy 69 thru Mosby
LEFT on Cameron Rd crossing Wornall and MO 92
RIGHT at Jesse James Farm Rd
LEFT into main entrance of Watkins Mills State Park
Cycle counter clockwise around the Lake on the north side
Exit the park through the same gate entered.
RIGHT on Jesse James Farm Rd into Kearney and Clem's Restaurant on Washington
Return south on MO 33 crossing Hwy 69 and becoming Hwy B
RIGHT on Hwy H to campus

SMITHVILLE TO GOWER

Starting Point: Smithville Shopping Center, Hwy 169 & KK

Distance: 58 miles

Degree of Difficulty: a great ride

Terrain: mostly flat except 4 miles of hills from Frazier to Gower

Things To See: combines both scenery and good food at Harmer's Cafe in Edgerton. Platte River valley is very scenic.

Cycle west on Hwy KK
RIGHT on Hwy B
RIGHT at Hwy E to Ridgely
North on Hwy B to Edgerton
LEFT on MO Z
RIGHT at Hwy F
RIGHT at MO 116
LEFT on Hwy E into Frazier
RIGHT on Hwy B into Edgerton and food at Harmer's Cafe
Continue east on Hwy Z
RIGHT at Hwy 169
LEFT at Hwy F past Trimble, the water tower on left
Stay right on Hwy F back to Smithville

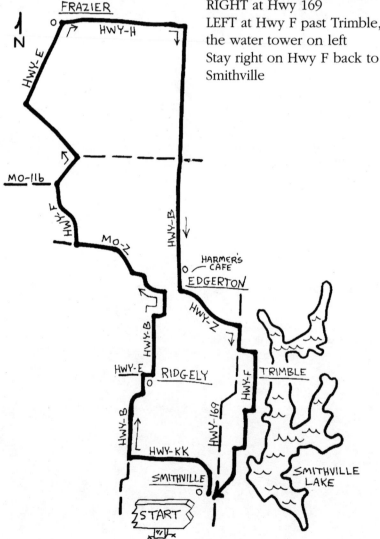

SMITHVILLE TO PLATTSBURG

Starting Point: Smithville Shopping Center, Hwy 169 & KK

Distance: 55 miles

Degree of Difficulty: moderate

Terrain: mostly flat north & south, hilly east & west

Things To See: scenic Platte River valley. Bert & Ernie's Restaurant in Plattsburg is good but closed on Sunday.

Cycle west on Hwy KK
RIGHT on Hwy B
RIGHT at Hwy E to Ridgely
LEFT at Hwy B
RIGHT on Hwy Z at Edgerton
LEFT on Hwy B - very hilly
RIGHT at MO 116 to Plattsburg
RIGHT at Hwy C
RIGHT on Hwy J
RIGHT on Hwy W
LEFT at Hwy F to Smithville

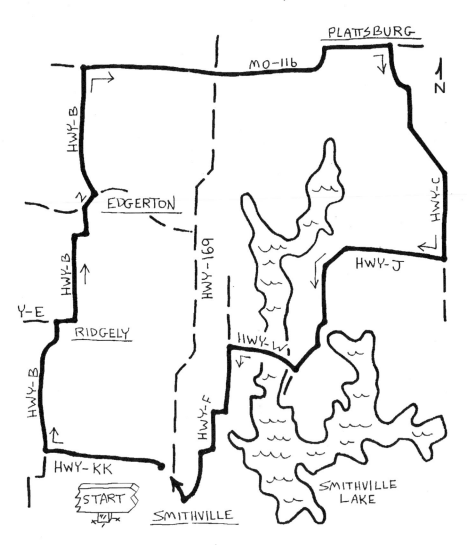

SMITHVILLE TO ST. JOSEPH

Starting Point: Smithville
Shopping Center, Hwy 169 &
KK
Distance: 80 miles
Degree of Difficulty: distance
makes this ride difficult
Terrain: mostly flat along
Platte River, east-west hilly
Things To See: Edgerton and
Agency very scenic. An
especially good fall
foliage ride.
Wiedmier's Restaurant
just off I-29 south of
St. Joe is recommend-
ed by Ken McFarland.

Cycle west o KK
RIGHT on B
LEFT at F
RIGHT at MO 116
LEFT on E
LEFT on H
RIGHT at FF to Wiedmier's
Restaurant

Return on FF
LEFT on H
RIGHT at E
RIGHT at MO 116
LEFT on F
Continue on Z
RIGHT at Hwy 169
LEFT at F to Smithville

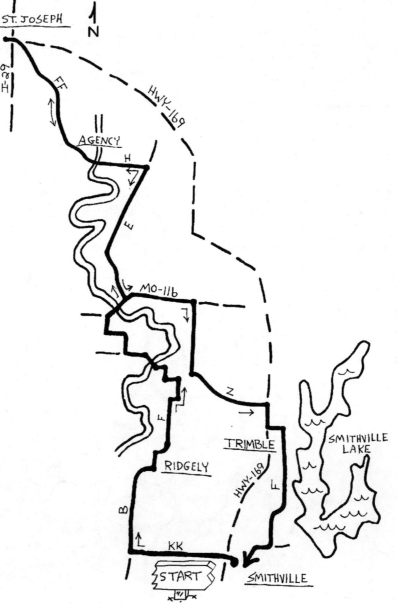

EXCELSIOR SPRINGS TO POLO

Starting Point: Crown Hill
Shopping Center, Excelsior
Springs
Distance: 60 miles
Degree of Difficulty: chal-
lenging
Terrain: moderately hilly
Things To See: Lawson, very
scenic Crooked River Valley,
Red River Inn at Polo

Cycle north on Hwy 69
RIGHT on Italian Way
LEFT at Salem Rd
RIGHT at Moss St
LEFT on Nolker which
becomes West St
RIGHT on 6th St at Casey's
East on Hwy D
LEFT at MO 13 into Polo and
The Red Rooster Inn
Return south on MO 13
RIGHT on Hwy D
LEFT at Hwy C
RIGHT at Hwy U
LEFT on Hwy M
RIGHT on MO 10 into
Excelsior Springs

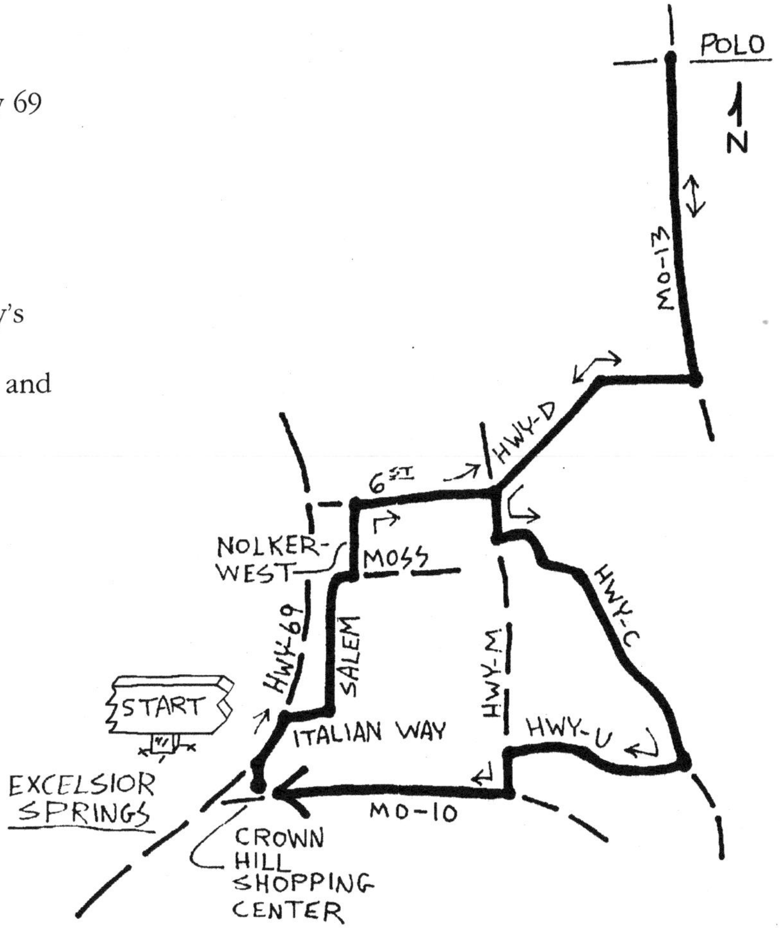

PLATTSBURG-MAYSVILLE LOOP

Starting Point: Plattsburg, MO, west of I-35 on Hwy 116
Distance: 60 miles
Degree of Difficulty: a good workout
Terrain: moderately hilly
Things To See: this is country, folks. This is a Dick Stephens ride so it's gotta be good.

Cycle east on Hwy 116
LEFT on Hwy 33
LEFT at Hwy 36
RIGHT at J
RIGHT on Hwy 6 north of Amity
RIGHT on Hwy 33 at Maysville
LEFT at T
RIGHT first road thru Turney
Contue N and then A
LEFT at Lathrop on Hwy 116 west to Plattsburg

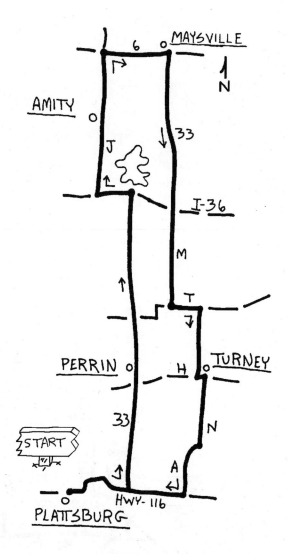

TIM OSBURN

publishes the monthly newsletter of the Kansas City Bicycle Club. He began cycling sometime prior to 1983 and today is interested in commuting by bicycle. Tim is a "free spirit" and is an important advocate of Northland cycling.

ART LOEPP

is always recognizable by his white beard. Art is an active Northland rider who seems to show up in out of the way places to ride like Tognanoxie, Lawrence, and RAGBRAI. He manages to teach school and to play a competitive game of tennis while logging substantial miles on his bicycle.

Page

1. Bonner to Lawrence (18,36,54)......................97

2. Tour of Tonganoxie (43,52) 98

3. Dave's Loop (20) 99

4. Bi-County Loop (62)................................100

5. Leavenworth-Wyandotte Lake (40)...................101

6. Roll Through Southern Platte County (32)........102

7. Parkville to Leavenworth (40).........................103

8. Tour of Seven Cities (44)..............................104

9. Farley to Atchison (60)............................... 105

10. Those HIlls of Missouri (40, 50) 106

11. Leavenworth-Weston-Atchison Loop (50)......... 107

12. Leavenworth to Weston (25) 108

13. The Barn B & B Overnight (36)..........................109

14. Nebraska and Back (44)...................................110

15. Easton Loop (30) 111

16. Winchester Loop (50).. 112

17. Weeknite Loops (15,21) 113

18. Buffalo Bill Metric (62)...................................... 114

19. Leavenworth-Wyandotte Loop (45)................... 115

20. Leavenworth-Tonganoxie Basehor Loop (45)....116

21. Leavenworth-Tonganoxie (38)..........................117

22. Leavenworth County Metric (62)...................... 118

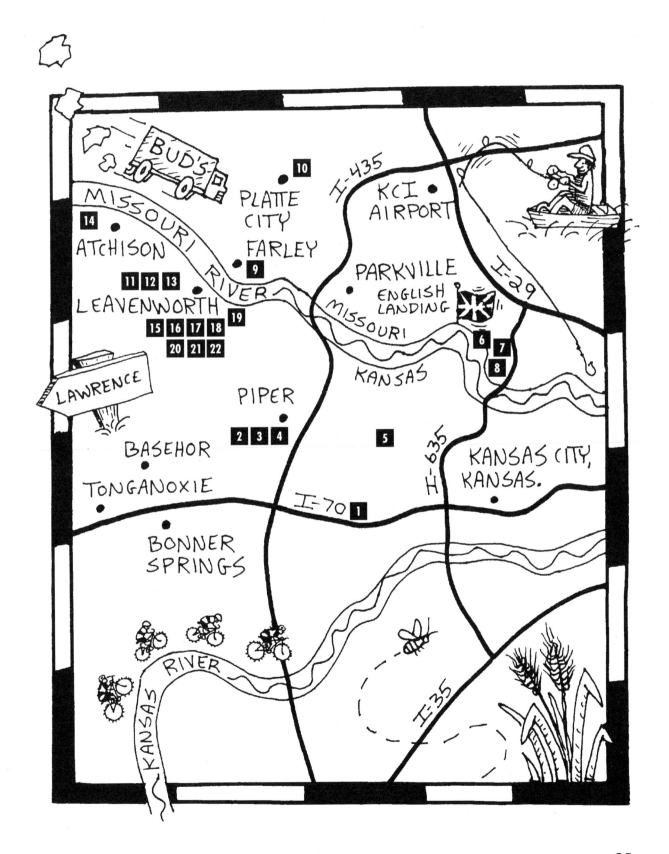

JOEL BUCK

is an active member of the Leavenworth Bicycle Club. Fortunately for Gregg Scircle and other Leavenworth cyclists, the military has landed Joel at Ft. Leavenworth. Both he and Gregg Scircle have provided many good rides from Leavenworth and would be happy to assist you in cycling the Leavenworth area.

GREGG SCIRCLE

of Leavenworth began cycling "seriously" in 1971. Gregg has been an active member and advocate of League of American Wheelmen (LAW) for more than 20 years. His career in cycling began with the Bluegrass Wheelmen in Lexington, Kentucky. In 1985 Gregg founded the Leavenworth Bicycle Club. His other activities include teaching and coaching soccer.

BONNER TO LAWRENCE

Starting Point: Piggly Wiggly in Bonner Springs

Distance: Round trip Eudora 18 miles, DeSoto 36 miles, & Lawrence 54 miles

Degree of Difficulty: moderate

Terrain: gently rolling

Things To See: Kansas University, Maria's for German food in DeSoto, and Casey's in Eudora; the Free State Brewery is good for food and drink in Lawrence but, remember, you have a 27 mile ride home.

Cycle west from Bonner
RIGHT on LV32
LEFT on LV2
LEFT at Rte 2 across river into DeSoto
RIGHT at Main St. with Maria's on right at K10

RIGHT on old K10 which becomes D442 into Eudora
Continue on D442 to "T"
RIGHT across railroad tracks onto gravel
LEFT on 15th to Massachusetts and main street Lawrence

Return the same way.

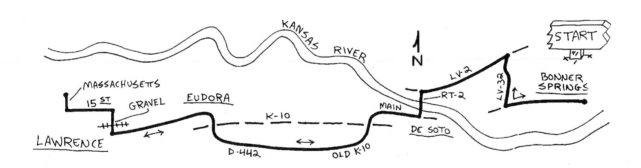

Starting Point: Piper High School, 110th north of Leavenworth Rd.
Distance: 43 miles and 52 miles
Degree of Difficulty:
Terrain: mostly flat
Things To See: Somewhat undeveloped and woodsy areas of Wyandotte and Leavenworth counties. And, there's probably something historical about Tonganoxie. Food and beverage in Basehor at Kelley's and in Tonganoxie.

Cycle south of Piper High School on 110th
RIGHT at Parallel
RIGHT at 155th (LV7) north for 4 miles
LEFT on Fairmont Rd (LV8)
RIGHT on LV5
43 Milers turn left on LV8/5 and another left on LV5 southwest to Tonganoxie.
Refer to return instructions from Tonganoxie at the end of this description.

52 Milers continue north on LV5
LEFT at LV10
LEFT at LV29 which becomes LV5 at LV8/5 intersection where routes rejoin
LEFT (south) at entry to Tonganoxie
RIGHT on Hwy 24/40
LEFT at Vet Clinic
LEFT on LV6 with 1 1/2 mile of gravel
LEFT at LV2 (158th)
RIGHT at Hwy 24/40
LEFT on 155th (LV7)
RIGHT on Parallel
LEFT at 110th to Piper High School

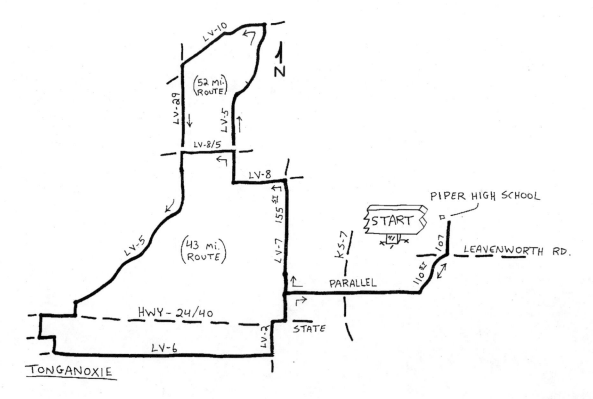

98

DAVE'S LOOP

Starting Point: 110th & Parallel, Wyandotte County
Distance: 20 miles
Degree of Difficulty: mildly challenging
Terrain: moderately hilly
Things To See: Basehor-Wolcott-Piper, rural bi-county ride

Dave Neff contributed this ride in the '92 book as a challenging course for those who don't have time for a longer tour.

Cycle west from 110th and Parallel
RIGHT on 155th (LV7) with a stop at either Casey's or Kelley's in Basehor
Continue north on 155th (LV7)
RIGHT on Fairmount downhill (LV8); Farm Market at corner of K7 and Fairmount

LEFT at 123rd for 2 mile uphill
RIGHT at K5 to Wolcott
RIGHT on Hutton Rd. which angles left and then turns into 110th south to Parallel

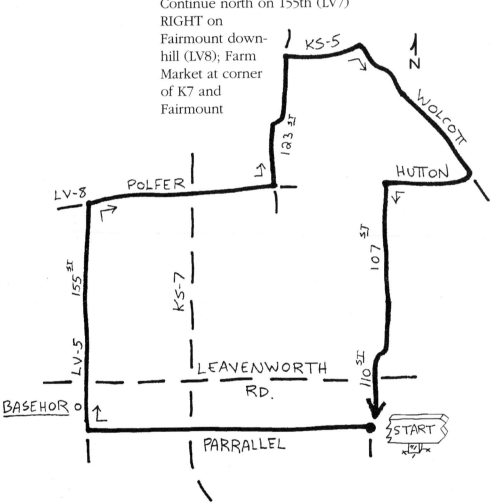

BI-COUNTY LOOP

Starting Point: 110th & Parallel, Wyandotte County
Distance: 62 miles
Terrain: moderately hilly
Things To See: some rural areas; rest stops in Basehor, McLouth, and Tonganoxie

Cycle west from 110th on Parallel
RIGHT at 155th north for 4 miles
LEFT at Fairmont Rd.(LV8)
RIGHT on LV5
RIGHT on Vilas
LEFT at 10th St
LEFT at K92 thru Springdale and McLouth to flashing red light
LEFT on K16 to Tonganoxie

OPTION:
east on LV5 through Jarbalo, right on LV7, and left on Parallel to start
Return east on LV6 with caution of 1/2 mile of gravel
LEFT at LV2
RIGHT at State Ave
LEFT on LV7 (155th)
RIGHT on Parallel to 110th

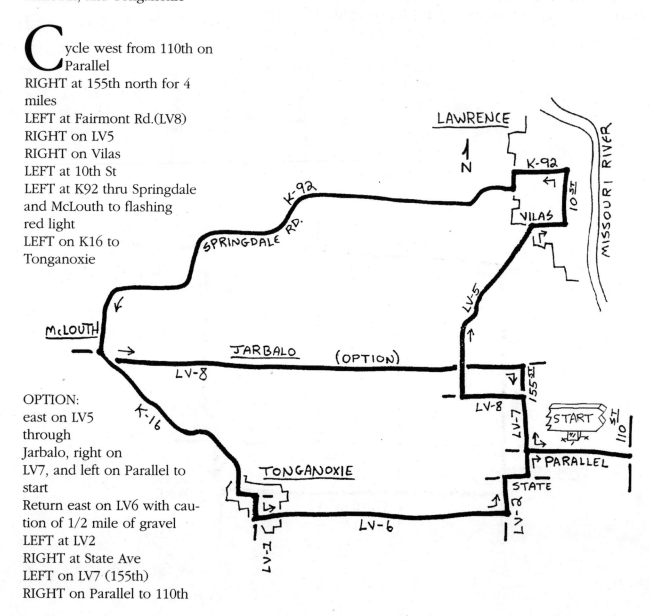

LEAVENWORTH-WYANDOTTE LAKE

Starting Point: Armed Forces Insurance Bldg, Eisenhower Blvd.(34th St.),Leavenworth
Distance: 40 miles
Degree of Difficulty: moderate
Terrain: K5 very hilly
Things To See: Wyandotte County, Wolcott, and Basehor

Cycle east on Eisehower(34th)
RIGHT on K5, very hilly, into Wolcott
RIGHT at 110th through Piper
RIGHT at Parallel across US73(K7)
RIGHT on LV7 at Basehor
LEFT on LV8
RIGHT at LV5
RIGHT at Eisenhower to starting point

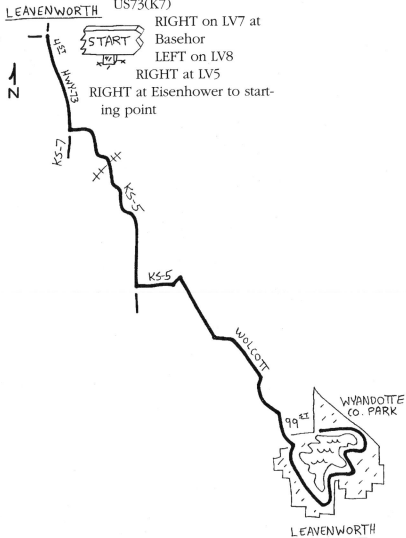

ROLL THROUGH SOUTHERN PLATTE COUNTY

Starting Point: English Landing in Parkville
Distance: 32 miles
Degree of Difficulty: moderate
Terrain: mostly rolling hills, with climbs when crossing river bluffs
Things To See: Historic downtown Parkville, Park College, English Landing. Can detour into Platte City by staying on Hwy N, rather turning on Hwy D. Hwy N is one of the prettier rides in Platte County as it twists and turns through he Platte River valley, past farm fields and tobacco barns.

Cycle from English Landing
LEFT on FF Hwy
RIGHT on K Hwy

LEFT at 152 Hwy
RIGHT at N Hwy
RIGHT on D Hwy (120th)
LEFT on Nevada
RIGHT at Prairie View
RIGHT at Mexico City
LEFT on Bern
LEFT on 291 Hwy
RIGHT at row of conifers in ditch along 291 Hwy. This is faint path to get to frontage road.
South at Prairie View (frontage road)
LEFT on Congress
RIGHT on 79th Place
LEFT at Mace
RIGHT at Lingley Dr
RIGHT on Eastside Dr
LEFT on Blair Rd
LEFT at Cross Rd
RIGHT at Melody (Cross Rd grdually veers right turning into Melody)

Cross Hwy 9 into Parkville Heights Shopping Center. Work your way to left and back of center.
RIGHT on 63rd St
LEFT on Bell Rd
LEFT at Hamilton
RIGHT at West St
LEFT on FF Hwy
Coast back to the park, explore the shops of Parkville the nature trail, and Park College campus.

PARKVILLE TO LEAVENWORTH

Starting Point: Parkville's English Landing (Farmer's Market)
Distance: 40 miles
Terrain: flat, follows the river
Things To See: Very scenic ride along the Missouri River; eat at the Pullman Restaurant in Leavenworth - "bicycle friendly". The Fort, the Federal Penitentiary, and old homes provide interesting sightseeing if you're not in a hurry.

This is a particularly delightful ride for beginning and intermediate cyclists. Not only is the ride itself not too challenging but there's plenty to see and do in Leavenworth.

Cycle from Parkville north on FF which parallels the bluffs on the right.
FF becomes gravel at the 5 mile mark for about 1.5 miles
LEFT on M45 just past Waldron
LEFT at Spur 45 about 2 miles north of Farley which becomes M92 and crosses the Missouri River bridge into Leavenworth. Extreme caution on the bridge.
LEFT on 4th St. to the Pullman Restaurant at 3rd & Delaware. After food, tour the homes on south Broadway.

Return to Parkville the exact route you came.

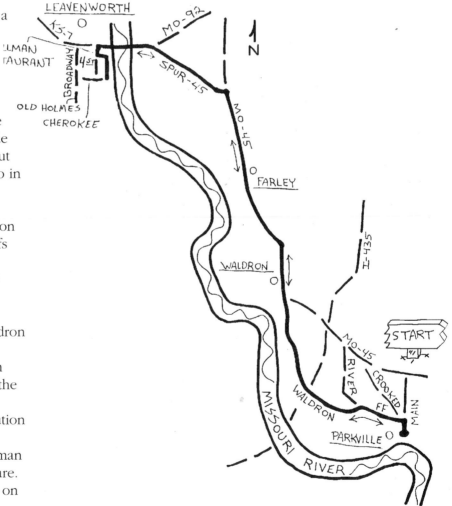

TOUR OF SEVEN CITIES

Starting Point: Parkville's English Land (Farmer's Market)
Distance: 44 miles
Degree of Difficulty: no problem. Some suggest an out and back route avoiding MO 45 traffic
Terrain: few hills around Platte City
Things To See: Often an organized ride but can be easily enjoyed with friends. Fannie's is a favorite spot to eat in Platte City. By the way, the seven cities are: Waldron, Farley, Beverly, Weston, Platte City, Kansas City, and Parkville.

Cycle north from Parkville on FF which parallels the bluffs on the right.
Continue on FF to 5 mile point where it becomes gravel for 1.5 miles
LEFT on M45 just after Waldron
Continue north on M45 to Farley and the Farley Grocery for Marshmallow Pepsi
M45 continues to the north and at Weston
RIGHT on J at the flashing yellow light for a 5 mile ride into Platte City
Fannie's for food is located at 3rd and Main
Cycle south from Platte City on 4th Street which becomes N
LEFT on T across I-435
RIGHT on K (Hampton Rd), also Union Chapel Rd
LEFT on FF and two more miles into Parkville

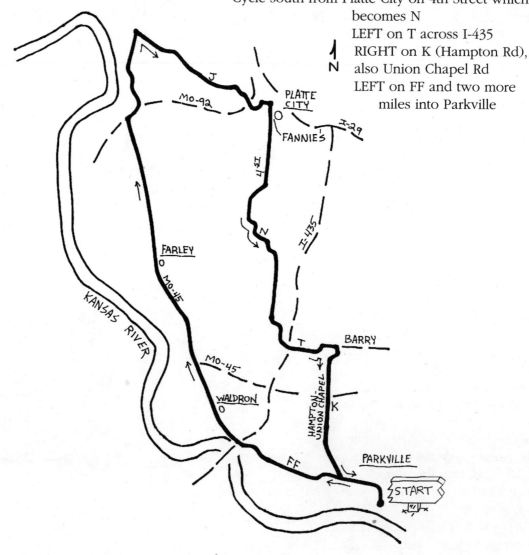

FARLEY TO ATCHISON

Starting Point: Farley Grocery, M 45 north of Parkville
Distance: 60 miles
Terrain: flat since it follows the river
Things To See: Farley Grocery offers Marshmallow Pepsi for those who think young. It's closed on Sunday. Both Atchison and Leavenworth have many old, charming homes. Stop by Nell Hills store in Atchison

This is an out and back trip for those cyclists fortunate to own bike racks. It's recommended crossing the Missouri River bridge at Leavenworth and then travelling the Kansas side north to Atchison to avoid the heavy traffic.

Cycle north from Farley on M 45 about two miles
LEFT on Spur 45 which becomes M 92 before crossing the Missouri River bridge at Leavenworth. Cross with extreme caution.
Once across the bridge, continue west on Metropolitan (Hwy 73) with a right at the Federal Penitentiary
North on scenic Hwy 73 all the way to Atchison (20 miles)
RIGHT on Main St. to Third St. and Paolucci's Restaurant.
Visit Nell Hills store and return exactly the same route.

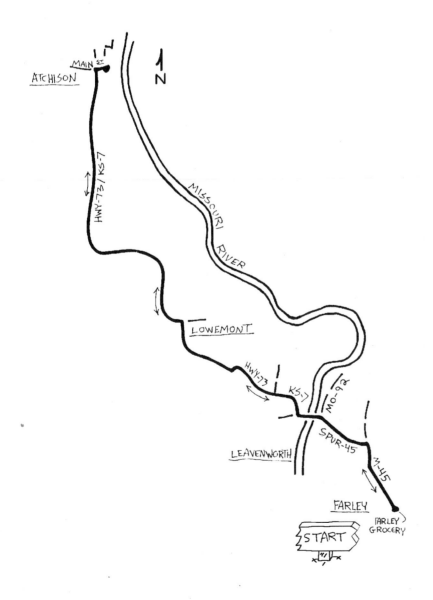

THOSE HILLS OF MISSOURI

Starting Point: Court House in Platte City

Distance: 40 & 50 miles
Degree of Difficulty: tough
Terrain: hilly
Things To See: Hills, hills, and more hills! Fannie's for food in Platte City, other stops in Dearborn, Edgerton, and Ridgely

Cycle northwest on Hwy 371
Longer option continue north on Hwy 371, RIGHT on Z, RIGHT on B
Shorter option RIGHT on E into Ridgely
RIGHT at B
LEFT at Hwy 92
RIGHT on C
RIGHT on 128th street across I-29
RIGHT on Running Horse Road to Hwy 92
LEFT to Court House in Platte City

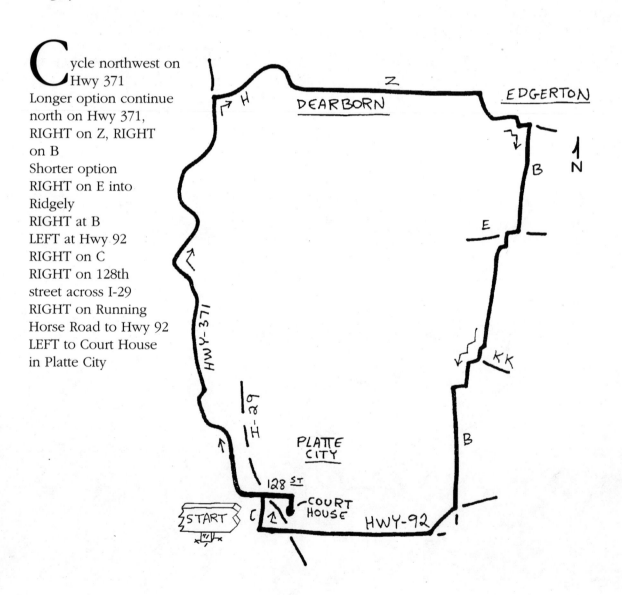

LEAVENWORTH-WESTON-ATCHISON LOOP

Starting Point: Park & Ride, Hwy 73, entrance to 35th Infantry, Fort Leavenworth

Distance: 50 miles

Degree of Difficulty: not difficult

Terrain: gently rolling, following the river

Things To See: beautiful countryside, stop at Nell Hills store in Atchison for a surprise, Weston offers endless pleasures.

Cycle northwest on US73 all the way to Atchison
Cross the river eastbound on US59
RIGHT on Mo45 past Weston
RIGHT on J into Weston
Continue south on Mo45
RIGHT on spur 45 across bridge to Leavenworth

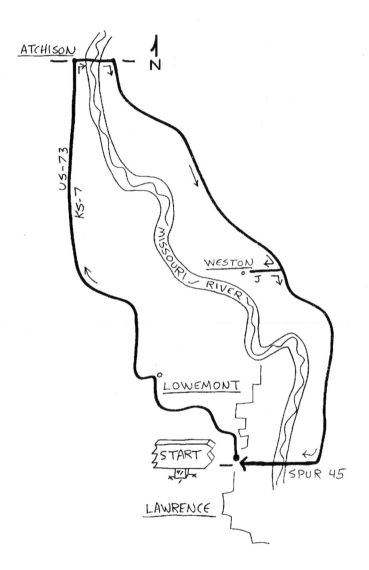

LEAVENWORTH TO WESTON

Starting Point: Park & Ride, US 73, entrance to 35th Infantry, Leavenworth
Distance: 25 miles
Degree of Difficulty: easy
Terrain: mostly flat until outskirts of Weston.
Things To See: Weston for its many fine restaurants, fun shopping, and B & Bs; try the Vineyard for gourmet dining. Weston is famous for tobacco and the McCormick Distillery. A truly charming ride with an exciting destination.

Cycle east on US 73 (Metropolitan) across Missouri River bridge; use extreme caution.
RIGHT at 45 spur
LEFT at Hwy 45 past Beverly
LEFT on Hwy J into Weston
Return the same way.

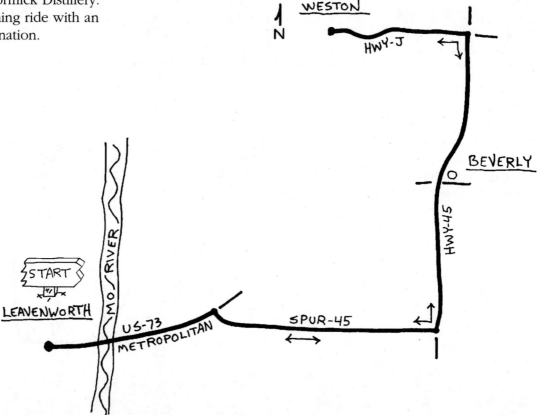

THE BARN B & B OVERNIGHT

Starting Point: Park & Ride, Hwy 73, entrance to 35th Infantry, Fort Leavenworth
Distance: 36 miles each way
Things To See: The Barn B & B in Valley Falls, KS (800-869-7717)

Cycle west on US 73 (Metropolitan)
RIGHT on LV 14 at west side of federal penitentiary
LEFT at Old US 73 (Santa Fe Trail)
LEFT at K192 thru Easton all the way to Valley Falls (also called K16 when crossing Hwy 59)
LEFT on K4 at Valley Falls to the Barn
Return the same route.

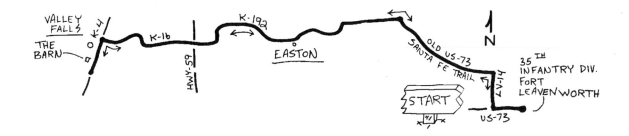

NEBRASKA AND BACK

Starting Point: Troy, Kansas, US73/K7 north
from Leavenworth thru Atchison to Troy
Distance: 44 miles
Degree of Difficulty: totally pleasurable
Terrain: gently rolling
Things To See: An out and back ride where
trees arch the road like the French countryside.
Stop for food in White Cloud. Troy was
the first stop in Kansas on the original
Pony Express. Attractions in Troy
include Doniphan County Courthouse
built of ntive limestone. The Tall Oak Indian
Monument by Peter Toth opposite the court-
house. This ride also passes the Iowa Sac and
Fox Indian Reservation. Thanks to Joel Buck of
Leavenworth for the ride.

Cycle north from Troy on KS7
20 miles north pass thru White Cloud
Continue another 2 1/2 miles across the
Nebraska border just to tell the folks back home.
Return the same route. No one ever gets lost on
this ride.

NEBRASKA

N

KANSAS

WHITE CLOUD

KS-7

TROY
START

US-73
K-7

EASTON LOOP

Starting Point: Bud's Warehouse, 20th & Spruce, Leavenworth
Distance: 30 miles
Degree of Difficulty: easy
Terrain: moderately hilly
Things To See: similar to Weeknite Loops ride with extra 9 mile loop

Cycle west on Spruce (K92)
15 mile cutoff option - RIGHT on LV33 and RIGHT on LV14
21 mile cutoff option - RIGHT on LV17 and RIGHT on K192, RIGHT on LV14
30 mile cutoff option - RIGHT on LV21 to Easton, RIGHT on K192, RIGHT on LV14

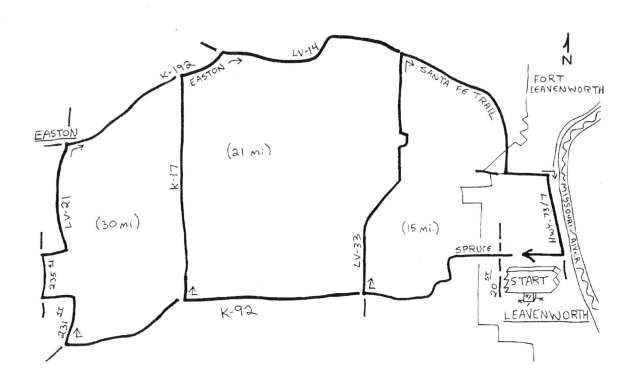

WINCHESTER LOOP

Starting Point: Bud's
Warehouse, 20th & Spruce,
Leavenworth
Distance: 50 miles
Degree of Difficulty: challeng-
ing
Terrain: hilly especially K192
Things To See: Cafe on Main
Street in Winchester; stop in
Easton

Cycle west on Spruce (K92)
After McLouth turnoff look for
RIGHT on unnamed road
LEFT at T into Winchester and
Cafe on Main St.
East on K192 through Easton
and over some hills
RIGHT on Santa Fe Trail
(LV14)
RIGHT on 20th to starting
point

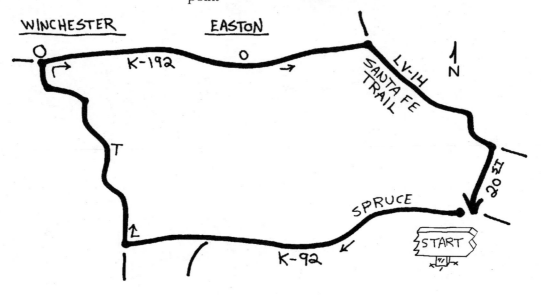

WEEKNITE LOOPS

Starting Point: Bud's Warehouse, 20th & Spruce, Leavenworth
Distance: 15 & 21 miles
Degree of Difficulty: not too challenging
Things To See: These are loops to be done as an evening workout during the week.

Cycle west from Bud's on Spruce which becomes K92
15 Mile Option
RIGHT at LV33
RIGHT at Military Drive (Old US 73) across Metropolitan
Continue south on 20th to starting point

21 Mile Option
Instead of right on LV33, continue west on K92
RIGHT at LV 17
RIGHT at K192
RIGHT at Military Drive (Old US 73) across Metropolitan
Continue south on 20th to starting point

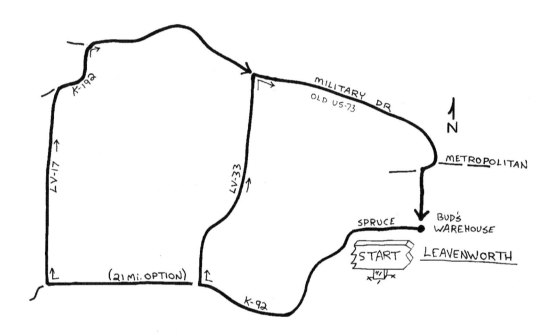

BUFFALO BILL METRIC

Starting Point: David Brewster Park, 18th & Ottawa, Leavenworth
Distance: 62 miles
Degree of Difficulty: a variety of challenges
Terrain: some hills
Things To See: Santa Fe Trail (Old 73), Easton, McLouth, Tonganoxie

A great way to see Leavenworth County without doing "hard time". The ride contibuted by Greag Scircle and Joel Buck, a couple of Buffalo Bill's buddies.

Cycle north on 20th St
RIGHT on US 73
LEFT at Santa Fe Trail (Old 73)
RIGHT at junction with US 73
LEFT on LV 14
LEFT on LV 13 to Easton
Continue south at LV 21
RIGHT at K 92 and stay left (south) into McLouth
LEFT and south on K 16 to Tonganoxie
Return north eat on LV 5 but stay left at intersection with County Shop
RIGHT at T on K92
LEFT at 20th St to Park.

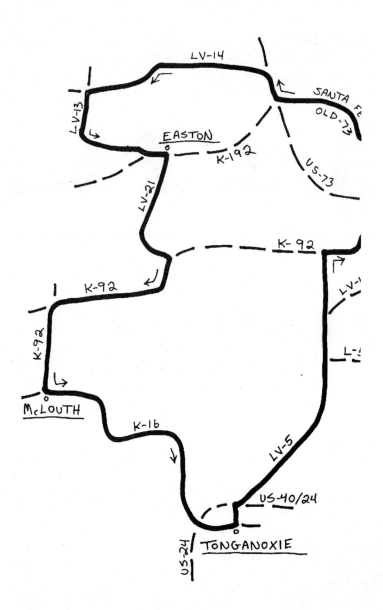

LEAVENWORTH-WYANDOTTE LOOP

Starting Point: Armed Forces Insurance Bldg, Eisenhower Blvd.(34th St.),Leavenworth
Distance: 40 miles
Degree of Difficulty: moderate
Terrain: K5 very hilly
Things To See: Wyandotte County, Wolcott, and Basehor

Cycle east on Eisehower(34th)
RIGHT on K5, very hilly, into Wolcott
RIGHT at 110th through Piper
RIGHT at Parallel across US73(K7)
RIGHT on LV7 at Basehor
LEFT on LV8
RIGHT at LV5
RIGHT at Eisenhower to starting point

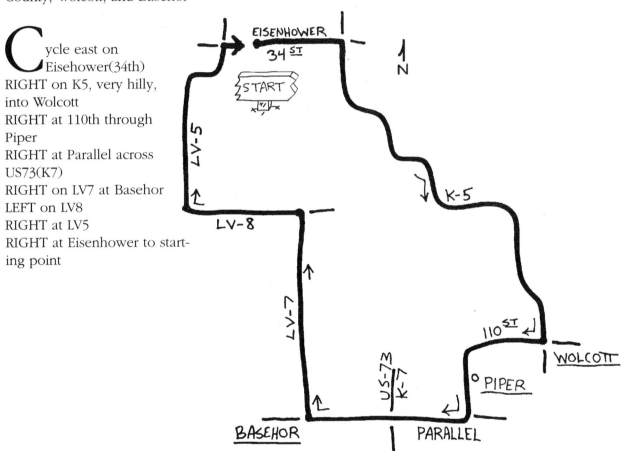

TONGANOXIE-BASEHOR LOOP

Starting Point: Armed Forces Insurance Bldg, Eisenhower Blvd.(LV34), Leavenworth
Distance: 45 miles
Degree of Difficulty: moderate
Terrain: LV5 hilly
Things To See: Kelley's Bar & Grill in Basehor, Ice Cream Shop in Tongie

Cycle west on 34th
LEFT on LV5
RIGHT at LV8
LEFT at LV5 into Tonganoxie intersection Main & Pleasant
LEFT (east) on LV6
LEFT on LV2 to Kelley's Bar & Grill in Basehor
LEFT at LV7
LEFT at LV8
RIGHT on LV5
RIGHT on Eisenhower(34th) to starting point

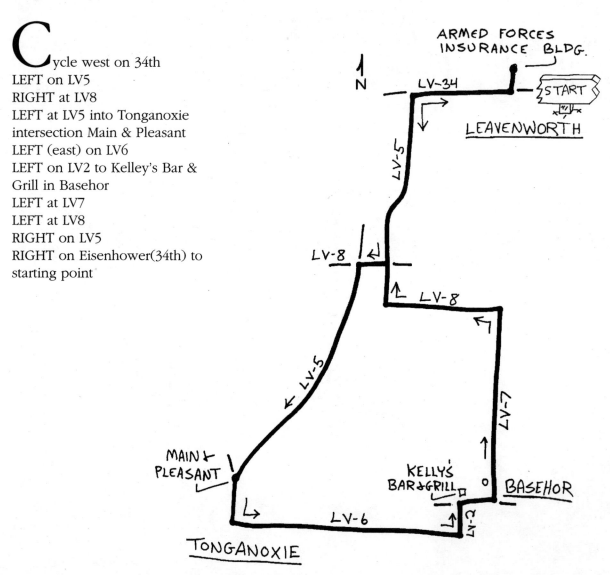

LEAVENWORTH-TONGANOXIE

Starting Point: Bud's Warehouse, 20th & Spruce, Leavenworth
Distance: 38 miles
Terrain: rolling hills
Things To See: Ice Cream shop in Tongie.

Cycle west on Spruce (K92)
LEFT on LV29
County Shop on left becomes LV5 into Tongi
Intersection of 2nd & Hwy 24/40 is Ice Cream Shop
Return the same way.

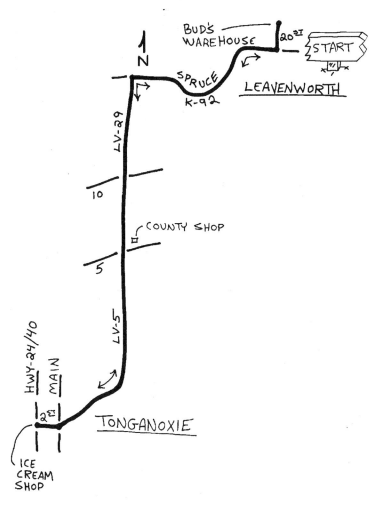

LEAVENWORTH COUNTY METRIC

Starting Point: Armed Forces Insurance Bldg, Eisenhower Blvd.(34th), Leavenworth
Distance: 62 miles
Degree of Difficulty: moderate
Terrain: rolling
Things To See: Kelley's Bar & Grill in Basehor, convenience store in Linwood, Ice Cream Shop in Tongie.

Cycle west on LV34
LEFT on LV5 which becomes LV8
LEFT at LV8
RIGHT at LV7 into Basehor
Cross Hwy 24/40 on LV21 becomes LV2
RIGHT on LV26
LEFT on LV32 into Linwood
RIGHT at LV25
LEFT at Hwy 24/40 into Tonganoxie to Pleasant & Main
RIGHT on LV5
LEFT on LV9
RIGHT at LV8
LEFT at LV29
RIGHT on LV10 which becomes LV34 to starting point

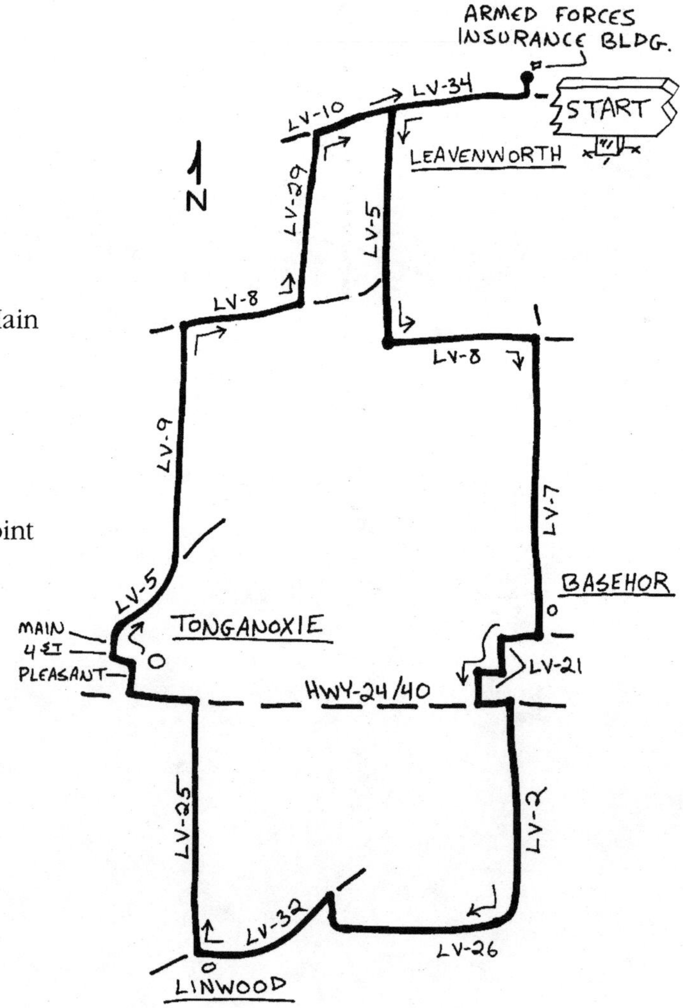

MAHLON STRAHM

a Lawrence area cyclist, made the transition from running to cycling in 1983. He has participated in all types of cycling from commuting, club rides, centuries, to USCF racing. Today, he enjoys mountain biking and tandem riding with his wife, Robbie.

JIM TURNER

is an important figure in Lawrence bicycling. Jim began cycling in 1975 and works diligently to make the Lawrence area a safer place to ride. He's been active in the Lawrence Bike Club and instrumental in the successes of the annual Lawrence classic bike ride, Octoginta.

Page

1. Lone Star Lake (30)..............................122

2. Lawrence To Vinland (20)...................123

3. Tongnoxie Tnago (35)........................124

4. Octoginta '94 (80)..............................125

5. Octoginta (80).....................................126

6. Lawrence To Lecompton (30)........... 127

7. Eudora In A Round About Way (37)..... 128

120

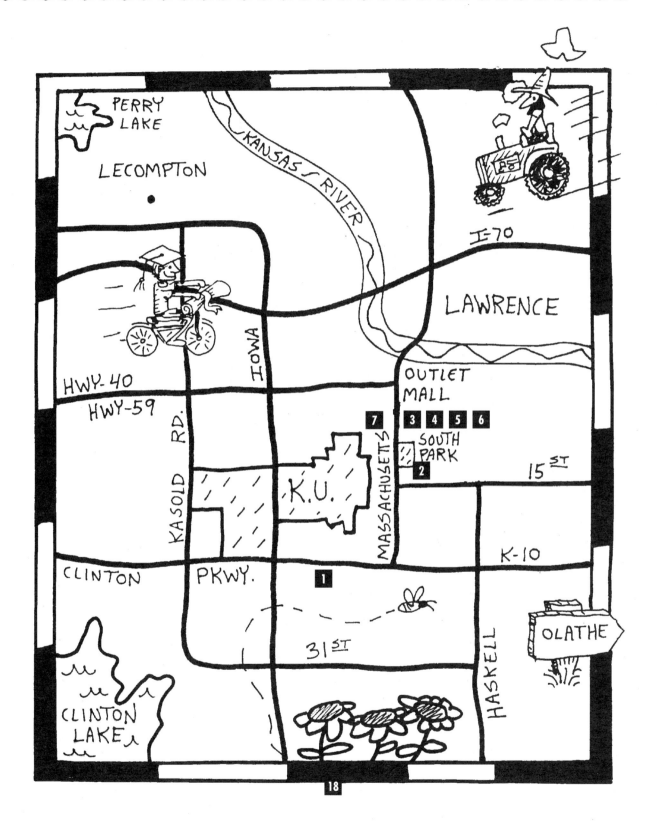

LONE STAR LAKE

Starting Point: Cycle Works
Bike Shop, 1601 W. 23rd,
Lawrence
Distance: 30 miles
Degree of Difficulty: easy
Terrain: flat to rolling hills
Things To See: Lone Star Lake

Start at Cycle Works Bike
Shop and head south on
Ousdahl
RIGHT at 26th Street
LEFT at Rosebud
RIGHT on 27th Street to Hwy
59 (same as Iowa)
Take frontage road on east
side to Crown Chevrolet
LEFT on Hwy 59
RIGHT at Douglas County 458
LEFT at D.C. 1039 to town of
Lone Star
Continue on 462 to 1031 and
Lone Star Lake.
Return the same route.

Ride by Jim Turner

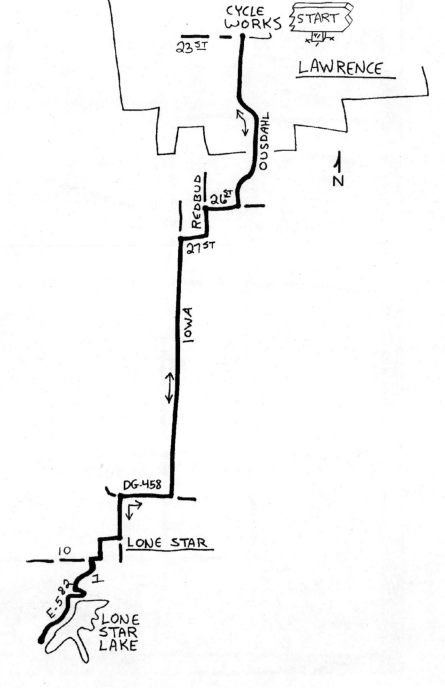

LAWRENCE TO VINLAND

Starting Point: South Park,
12th & Massachusetts,
Lawrence
Distance: 20 miles
Degree of Difficulty: easy
Terrain: flat to rolling

From South Park cycle east
on 12th Street
RIGHT on Haskell Avenue
which becomes D.C. 1055
Follow D.C. 1055 southeasterly
to Vinland

OPTION: Continue south on
1055 to Baldwin City by going
up Palmyra hill and adding 10
extra miles to the journey

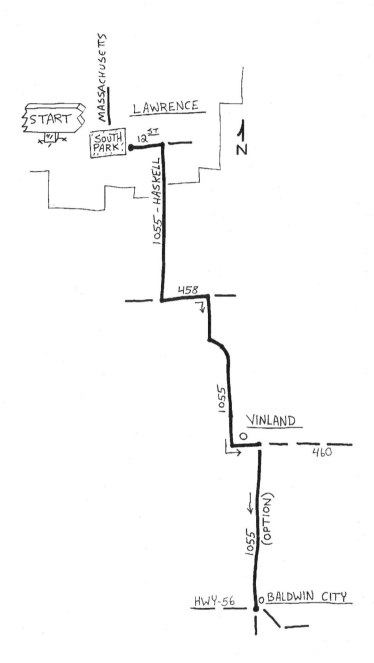

TONGANOXIE TANGO

Starting Point: South Park, 12th & Massachusetts, Lawrence
Distance: 35 miles
Degree of Difficulty: moderate
Terrain: flat to rolling hills

Exit South Park with a left onto Rhode Island
LEFT on 7th at Mall
RIGHT at New Hampshsire
LEFT at 6th
RIGHT on Massachusetts across bridge
RIGHT on Elm immediately after bridge
LEFT at 7th Street
RIGHT at Hwy 24/40
RIGHT on Hwy 32 for about 5 miles
LEFT on Leavenworth Road across I-70 into Tonganoxie
Stop at Bitlers and return the same route

Ride by Jim Turner

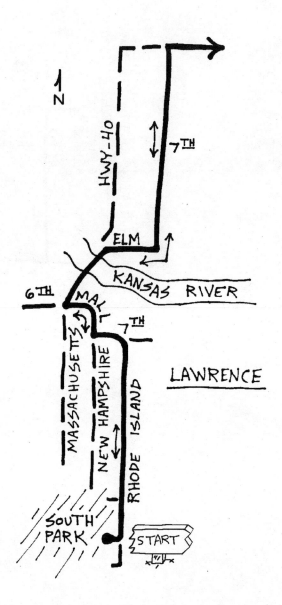

124

OCTOGINTA '94

Starting Point: South Park gazebo, 12th & Massachusetts, Lawrence
Distance: 80 miles
Degree of Difficulty: moderate to difficult
Terrain: rolling hills

Octoginta is one of the area's oldest and largest recreational bicycling events. For 26 years cyclists sign up for this fall classic which they consider the traditional wind-up event of the year.

The weekend was started by Bob and Joyce Salanke. Salanke, a former classical language professor at KU, created the name. Originally, it was 'Octiginta,' which referred to the 80 miles. It's much more than a bike ride, it's a weekend to commemorate another year of cycling.

Realizing not many enjoy an 80 mile ride on just any weekend, we recommend you try an out and back to Lake Perry or any point along the way.
Cycle north from South Park on New Hampshire
LEFT on 7th St
RIGHT on Michigan
LEFT at Riveridge Rd
RIGHT on Iowa
LEFT on DG 438
RIGHT at DG 1029 to Lecompton
Continue north to Perry
LEFT at 426A

RIGHT on K237 past Rock Creek Park
RIGHT (East) along south shore of Perry Lake past Perry Park
LEFT across Perry Lake on FAS 1280
RIGHT on K92 to Oskaloosa
RIGHT on US 59
LEFT at K92-16

RIGHT at DG 1045 for a ride back to the starting point. If the wind is out of the north, the return should be fast and easy.

Ride by Lawrence Bike Club & Mike Bryan

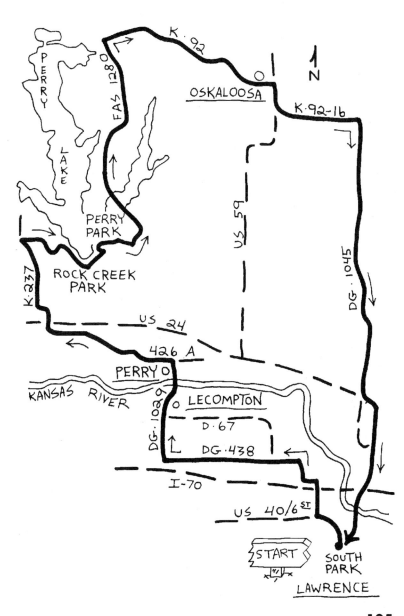

OCTOGINTA '93

Starting Point: South Park,
12th & Massachusetts,
Lawrence
Distance: 80 miles
Degree of Difficulty: always
challenging
Terrain: rolling
Things To See: Haunted
Church in Stull, Clinton Lake,
& Perry Lake

Cycle north from South
Park 12th &
Massachusetts, across river
At Hwy 24, continue north on
DG 1045 which become
Wellman Rd
LEFT at Hwy 92-16
RIGHT at U.S. 59 into
Oskaloosa
LEFT on Hwy 92
LEFT on FAS 1280 across Perry
Lake to town of Perry
RIGHT after crossing
Kansas River on DG 1023
past Lecompton
Take Hwy 40
RIGHT at 29th
LEFT at Stubbs Rd
LEFT at DG 442
RIGHT at Stull on DG 1023
Continue south around south-
ern part of Clinton Lake on
DG 458
LEFT on Hwy 59
RIGHT on 31st Street
LEFT in to South Park

Ride by Lawrence Bike Club &
Mike Bryan

LAWRENCE TO LECOMPTON

Starting Point: South Park, 12th & Massachusetts, Lawrence
Distance: 30 miles
Degree of Difficulty: moderte to difficult
Terrain: flat to rolling
Things To See:

Cycle north on Massachusetts
LEFT on 7th Street
RIGHT at Maine
LEFT at 5th Street
RIGHT on Arkansas
LEFT on 2nd which becomes Princeton Blvd. when crossing Iowa
RIGHT at Kasold Rd
LEFT at Lakeview Road (DG 438)
RIGHT on 1029 to Lecompton. Return the same route

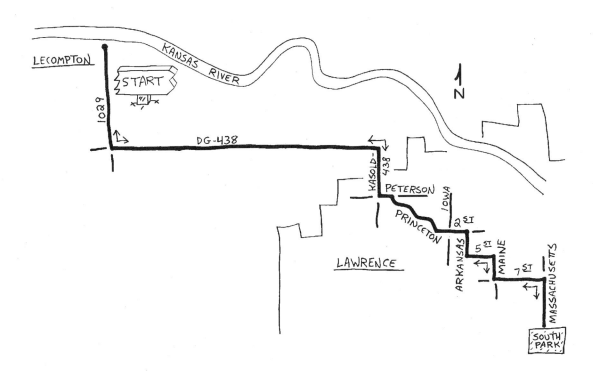

EUDORA IN A ROUND ABOUT WAY

Starting Point: 14th & Louisiana, KU campus, Lawrence
Distance: 37 miles
Degree of Difficulty: ride counterclockwise is winds are from south & clockwise if winds from north
Terrain: rolling as in river
Things To See: (A) Teepee, (B) Old Pilla House, (C) Dari-Treat, (D) Coal Creek Library and Vinland Airport

Cycle east on 14th
LEFT on Massachusetts across bridge
RIGHT on Elm immediately after bridge
LEFT at 7th Street
RIGHT at Hwy 24/40 which becomes K-32 at Leavenworth county line
RIGHT on Leavenworth County Road across Kansas River into Eudora for a rest stop
Continue south on D1061

RIGHT on D460 to Vinland
RIGHT at D1055
LEFT at D458
RIGHT on D1055 and turn left(west) at first main road
RIGHT on Louisiana across the Wakarusa River and follow it back to KU campus at 14th Street

Originally prepared by Mt Oread Bicycle Club in 1973

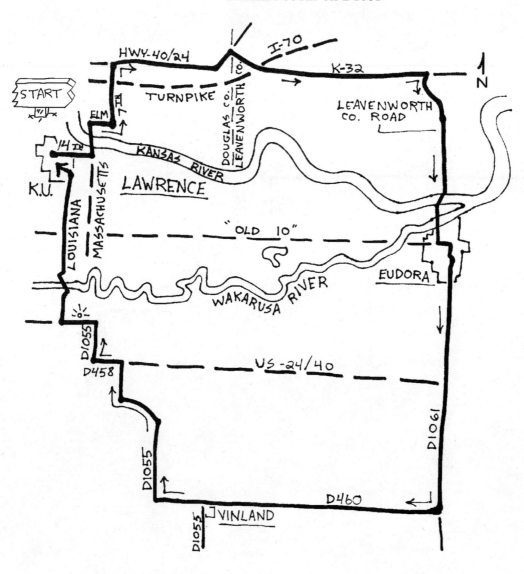

		Page
1.	Biking Across Kansas (BAK)	130
2.	Battle of Westport Ride (32)	131
3.	Wheel to Weston (35, 50, 100)	133
4.	Bagel & Bagel Ride #1 (12)	134
5.	Bagel & Bagel Ride #2	135

BIKING ACROSS KANSAS (BAK)

BIKING ACROSS KANSAS(BAK) is an annual 8-day classic created and still directed by Larry and Norma Christie of Wichita. In Christie's words, "BAK is not an endurance contest, a race, or a test of stamina. It is a recreational and social rally." The ride is always the second week in June from Saturday to Saturday. BAK is such a popular event that registration deadline is a month in advance. The number of riders is limited to about 300 on each of the three routes.

BAK '95, June 10-17, starts at the Colorado-Kansas border. There are three routes: the Bodacious Route, the Alluring Route, and the Kolossal Route. All 3 routes join together in Parsons, KS and continue together for the finish in Pittsburgh, KS after almost 500 miles.

Plan now to ride BAK next year. Entry forms will be available through area bike shops or by calling Larry and Norma Christie (316) 684-8184. There are two classic bicycling events in our area that have survived the test of time - BAK and OCTOGINTA.

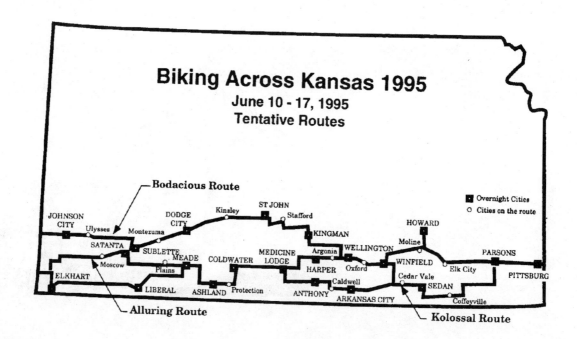

BATTLE OF WESTPORT RIDE

Starting Point: Westport Road & Pennsylvania, Kansas City, Mo.
Distance: 32 miles

This map from "The Battle of Westport" is printed with the permission of The Westport Historical Society. The 25 historical markers are the work of the Howard N. Monnett Memorial Fund. Additional information on the Battle of Westport and the Civil War in the Kansas City area may be obtained by calling (816) 931-6620.

Caution: this is designed as an automobile tour so discretion in choice of routes is advised.

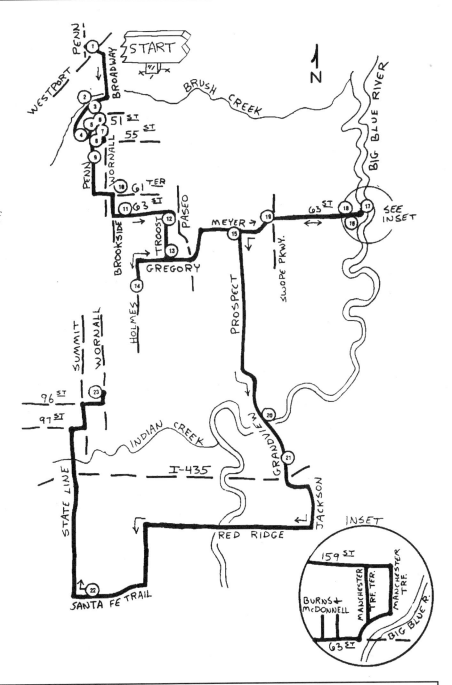

The Battle of Westport took place on October 21-23, 1864. General Sterling Price led 12,000 Confederate cavalrymen into Missouri on September 19th near Doniphan. After failing to capture St. Louis and Jefferson City, Price advanced toward Kansas and Fort Leavenworth. General Samuel R. Curtis with 20,000 Kansas State Militia and U.S. Volunteers, comprising the Army of the Border, met Price's Army of Missouri in what is now the Loose Park area. Union General Alfred E. Pleasanton,who had been chasing Price across Missouri with 7,000 cavalry,caught up with Price, and by routing Rebel General John S. Marmaduke at Byram's Ford, hit Price's right flank and rear. The defeated Confederates retreated South on the old Military Road. This tour covers the fighting on the 22nd, and 23rd of October, west of the Big Blue River.

1. Tour starts at Westport Road and Pennsylvania Avenue in Kansas City, Mo. "ACTION BEFORE WESTPORT - PRICE'S RAID" - Go east, right on Broadway and continue on J.C. Nichols Parkway across Brush Creek and right on Ward Parkway and left on Sunset Drive.

2. "UNION POSITION" - Continue southwest on Sunset Drive to Rockwell Lane.

3. "BATTLE OF WESTPORT" - Continue southwest on Sunset, left on 55th Street to address 1032.

4. "BENT & WARD HOUSES" - Continue east on 55th, left on Summit, bear right, and right on 51st St.

5. "CONFEDERATE POSITION" - East on 51st, right on Wornall and first right into Loose Park

6. "UNION ARTILLERY" - Continue on Park Drive, right on Wornall to intersection of 53rd Street

7. "McGHEE'S CHARGE" - Continue on Wornall, right on 55th Street to Pennsylvania. Dismount and walk north 100 yards

8. "BATTLE OF WESTPORT (MAP MARKER)" - Also here is a display of eight narrative plaque and a Parrott cannon barrel. Go south on Pennsylvania to 56th Street.

9. "COLLINS BATTERY" - South on Pennsylvania, left on 61st Terrace to Wornall

10. "WORNALL HOUSE" - 61st Street Terrace - Continue east, right on Brookside Boulevard and left on 63rd to Walnut

11. "HINKLE'S GROVE" - Continue east on 63rd to near Paseo Boulevard

12. "BATTLE OF THE BIG BLUE" - Right on Paseo, right on Meyer Boulevard, left on Troost and left into Forest Hills Cemetery to marker near entrance.

13. "SHELBY'S LAST STAND" - Proceed east on Central, turn right on Ravine to visit the Confederate Monument in the cemetery. Return to entrance then left on Troost and right on Gregory, and left on Holmes to address 7850

14. "MOCKBEE FARM" - Return north on Holmes, right on Gregory, left on Paseo and right on Meyer to Wabash

15. "HARRISONVILLE ROAD (PROSPECT)" - Continue on Meyer, left on Swope Parkway, right on 63rd Street and left on Manchester Trafficway, then 150 yards to No.16

16. "BATTLE OF WESTPORT" - Continue 100 yards to No.17 and dismount

17. "BATTLE OF THE BIG BLUE (MAP MARKER)" - Continue on Manchester Trafficway and left on 59th Street 200 yards beyond railroad track to No.17B

17B. "LOG HOUSE AND DEFENSE LINE" - Return 150

yards, right on Manchester Trafficway Terrace, right on Manchester Trafficway, right on 63rd and right at first driveway to No.17A near flagpole at Burns & McDonnell.

17A. "PRATT'S ARTILLERY" - Return to 63rd Street and turn right 100 yards to No.18

18. "BATTLE OF WESTPORT" - Continue on 63rd Street then left on Swope Parkway and go 75 yards

19. "BOSTON ADAMS HOUSE" - Continue on Swope Parkway, right on Meyer, left on Prospect, jog right and then left at Highway 71, then turn right within 50 yards, continue on Propect across the Big Blue River to No.20

20. "RUSSELLS FORD" - Continue on Prospect across Blue River Road, continue on Grandview Road to 98th Terrace; No.21 is 25 yards to the left

21. "NEW SANTA FE ROAD" - Continue on Grandview Road, right on Jackson, right on Red Bridge Road, left on Holmes, and right on Santa Fe Trail to near State Line

22. "NEW SANTA FE" - Continue west on Santa Fe Trail and right on State Line Road, right on 97th Street, left on Summit, and right on 96th Terrace to Wornall

23. "THOMAS FARMHOUSE" - end of tour

WHEEL TO WESTON

Starting Point: City Market, 5th & Walnut, Kansas City, MO
Distance: 35, 50, & 100 miles
Degree of Difficulty: easy, moderate, & difficult
Terrain: route up and back follows the river and is flat; hilly around Weston
Things To See: Missouri's backroads, tobacco fields, apple orcahrds, and historic Weston.

This is an annual ride sponsored by American Diabetes Association. It's held each year on Father's Day and attracts crowds of more than 1200 riders. The food, music, and support along the way is a bonus. The 35 and 50 mile riders can be back in Kansas City by noon. A new century (100 miles) route has been added. Registration information is available in all KC area bike stores.

The ride can be done for enjoyment at anytime, especially on weekends. Part of the route is heavily trafficked and therefore safer in a larger group. It's advisable to start from Parkville's English Landing rather than the City Market.

Cycle east on 3rd St
LEFT across Heart of America Bridge
Continue on Burlington (Hwy 9) to Parkville
Continue on Hwy FF with .5 mile gravel stretch
LEFT at Hwy 45 past Waldron with stop at Farley
Continue north on Hwy 45 past Beverly
Century Riders turn right thru Tracy (see insert)

Continue north on Hwy 45 past Weston Bend State Park
35 mile riders left on Hwy P
50 mile riders continue on Hwy 45
RIGHT at intersection, Kings Rd & Hwy H
RIGHT at Hwy P and follow into Weston

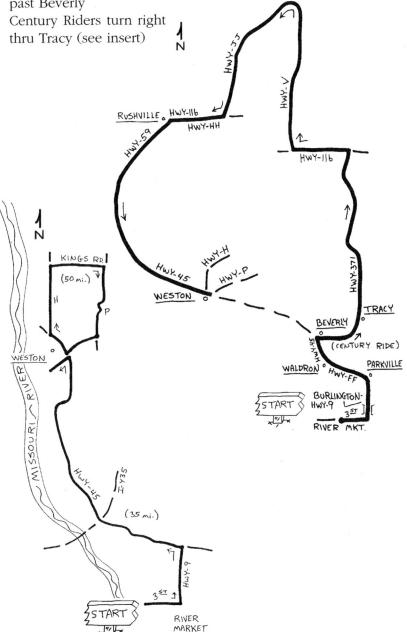

133

BAGEL & BAGEL RIDE #1

Starting Point: Bagel & Bagel, 3939 W 69th Terr, Prairie Village
Distance: 12 miles

Cycle east on Tomahawk across Mission Rd
RIGHT on 69th St
LEFT at Valley Rd
RIGHT at Meyer Blvd
LEFT on Brookside Plaza - Bagel & Bagel

LEFT on 63rd
RIGHT on Brookside Blvd
LEFT at 51st
RIGHT at Wornall through The Plaza
RIGHT on 47th
LEFT on Wornall
LEFT at Pennsylvania into Westport
LEFT at Westport Rd to Bagel & Bagel, 556 Westport Rd

Return west on Westport Rd
LEFT on Holly
RIGHT at 45th
LEFT at Wyoming
RIGHT on 51st becoming 50th
LEFT on Belinder
RIGHT at Mission Drive
RIGHT at Indian Lane
RIGHT on 63rd
LEFT on Indian Lane
RIGHT at 66th St
LEFT at Mission Rd into Prairie Village

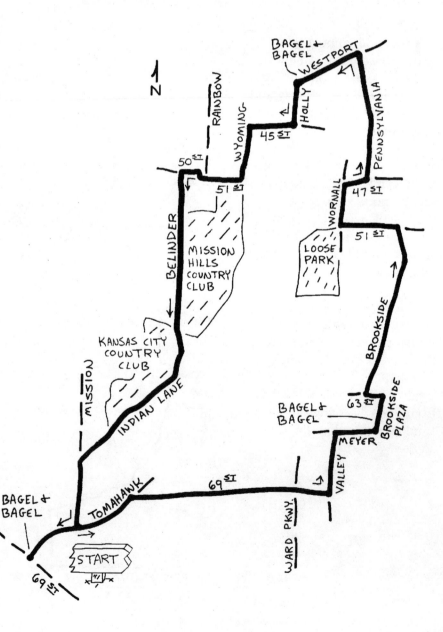

BAGEL & BAGEL RIDE #2

Starting Point: Bagel & Bagel, 3939 W 69th Terr, Prairie Village

Cycle southwest on Tomahawk Rd
RIGHT on Ash
LEFT at 73rd St
LEFT at Nall across 75th St
RIGHT on Tomahawk
LEFT on Dearborn across 79th and up a hill
Becomes Woodson at 83rd St
RIGHT at 87th Terrace
LEFT on Horton across 91st (with extreme caution)
Stay left on Outlook across 95th becomes Horton across 103rd
RIGHT at Indian Creek Drive
LEFT at Lamar and continue south across College
RIGHT on 115th across Metcalf (the light seems to change once daily)
RIGHT on Marty
LEFT at 112th
RIGHT at Lowell across College Blvd
LEFT on 110th to Bagel & Bagel, 8600 College Blvd

Cycle north on Mackey
LEFT at 108th Terrace crossing Antioch, becoming Indian Creek Pkwy
RIGHT at North Park to Indian Creek Trail eastbound
Follow the trail through Roe Park, across Roe Ave, by Suburban Nursery, where it becomes Tomahawk Creek

Trail
Exit the Tomahawk Trail at the soccer fields, 119th & Tomahawk Pkwy
Cycle west on 119th to Roe, and Bagel & Bagel in Hawthorne Plaza

Return to Prairie Village on Roe
RIGHT on Tomahawk Rd to starting point

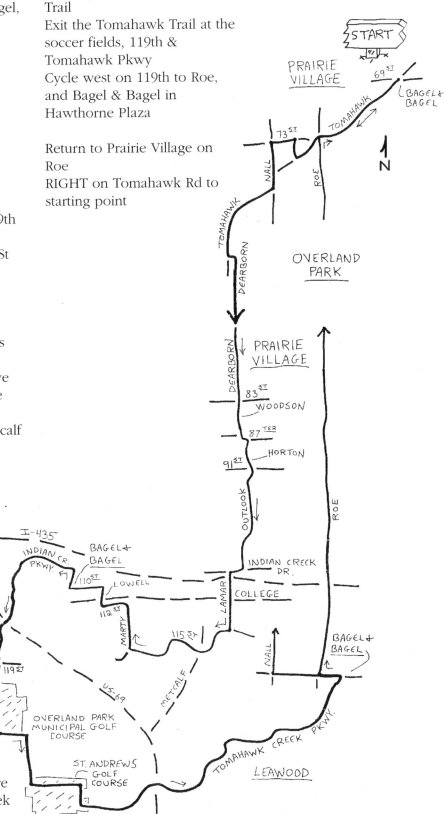

Page

1. Mountain Biking aka Off Road Cycling.............137

2. Rules of the Trail 138

3. Bluffwoods State Forest 139

4. Clinton State Park 140

5. Hillsdale Lake...141

6. Indian Cave State Park 142

7. Knob Knoster State Park 143

8. Lawrence Riverfront Trail............................ 144

9. Minor Park 145

10. Shawnee Mission Park 146

11. Smithville Lake....................................... 147

12. Weston Bend State Park 148

MOUNTAIN BIKING aka OFF ROAD CYCLING

Here in the Midwest we must be content with OFF ROAD CYCLING in lieu of MOUNTAIN BIKING. In the 1992 edition of Guide To Cycling Kansas, there was no mention of Off Road Cycling. Sales only three seasons ago were sharply in favor of the road bike. Today, road bikes probably account for less than ten per cent of mountain bike sales.

Why this sudden love affair with fat tire, muddy bikes rather than sleek, speedy road bicycles? The philosopher, Nietzsche, never contemplated a bicycle of any kind when he said of life, "Believe me! The secret of reaping the greatest fruitfulness and the greatest enjoyment from life is to live dangerously."

It's not our place to analyze the demographics of mountain biking. In sharing these "legal" trails with you, we ask that you obey the Rules of the Trail.

Mountain biking on public trails is a privilege. Follow the International Mountain Bicycling Association (IMBA) Rules of the Trail and everyone will enjoy the trails for many years. One irresponsible act can ruin mountain biking for all.

(IMBA RULES OF TRAIL CARTOONS) ©1992 Curt Evans & IMBA

Leave No trace!

Ride on open trails only!

Control your bicycle!

Always yield trail!

Plan ahead!

Never spook animals!

NATIONAL OFF-ROAD BICYCLE ASSOCIATION (NORBA)

This organization serves as another national governing organization for mountain biking. NORBA focuses primarily on off-road racing. To receive additional information or apply for membership (annual fee $25.00) write: NORBA, One Olympic Plaza, Colorado Springs, CO 80909 (719)578-4717

INTERNATIONAL MOUNTAIN BICYCLING ASSOCIATION (IMBA)

This organization promotes mountain bicycling opportunities through environmentally and socially responsible use of the land. To receive more information or apply for membership contact: IMBA, P.O. Box 412043, Los Angeles, CA 90041 (818)792-8830

BLUFFWOODS STATE FOREST

Located just south of St. Joseph, this is a rare forest preserve.

It's just an hour north of Kansas City on I-29 past KCI Airport to exit 20. Hwy 273 north and west . Right on Hwy 45. North on Hwy 59 to "State Forest" sign in Halls. Only 9 miles south of St. Joseph, this area is not a state park but a conservation area. Only the horse trail (not the hiking trails) may be used for cycling. The horse trail is approximately a 3 mile very hilly loop and the terrain is rugged.

Make certain you understand which trails are for cycling use. Any violations, intentional or otherwise, will cause the District Forester to close the area to cyclists. For further information, contact John Fleming, District Forester, (816-271-3100)

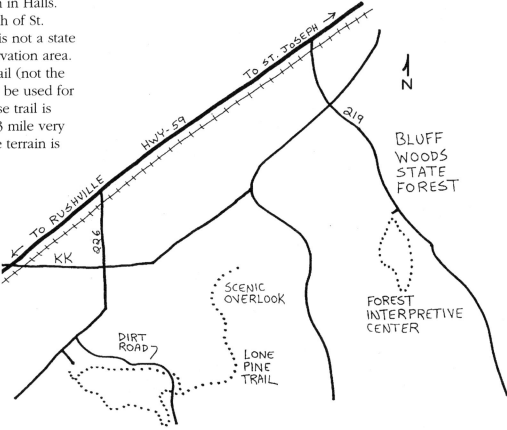

CLINTON STATE PARK

Clinton Lake, southwest of Lawrence, is less than one hour from Kansas City and only a short ride by car or by bicycle from Lawrence west via Clinton Pkwy.

If you're driving from the west, take Hwy 40. For additional information, contact Carl Ringler, Kansas Trails Council coordinator for Clinton Lake at 913-843-9141.

The mountain bike trail at Clinton State Park is considered very competitive. This trail and others are maintained through the efforts of the Kansas Trail Council.

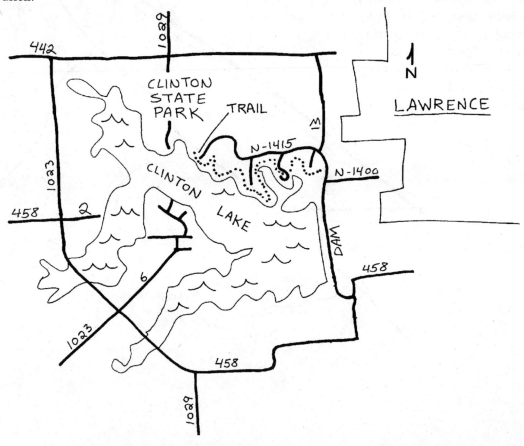

HILLSDALE LAKE

HILLSDALE LAKE (Miami County) is an exceptional natural resource not familiar to many Kansas City area cyclists. This 8000 acre facility, more than half of which is water, is located 40 miles south of Kansas City and only 9 miles from Paola.

In addition to the hunting, fishing and water sports facilities one would expect, Hillsdale Lake has campsites and equestrian trails usable as mountain bike trails as long as the rules of the trail are observed.

Additional information may be obtained by contacting Gary Lucas or Tim Schaid, Hillsdale State Park, (913) 783-4507

INDIAN CAVE STATE PARK

Indian Cave State Park is named for the hugh sand-stone cavity that is the main geologic feature of the area. The park covers some 3,000 acres, mostly timberland, and is bordered on the east by the Missouri River.

It's a 2 1/2 - 3 hour drive from Kansas City on I-29 north past KCI Airport
Exit at Squaw Creek, west on Hwy 159 through Rulo, NE
North at Falls City, NE
West on 73, north on 67, & follow signs to Indian Cave State Park (402) 755-2284
The horse trails may be shared with bicycles with the usual warnings that the horses have the right of way. There are extensive camping facilities.

NORTH RIDGE TRAIL

ST. DEROIN

N

PARK

67 73

NE
FALLS HWY-159
CITY

SQUAW
CREEK   KCIA

MISSOURI RIVER

ROCK BLUFF RUN

PAVED ROADS

INDIAN CAVE

HARDWOOD TRAIL

KNOB KNOSTER STATE PARK

Knob Knoster State Park is little more than an hour's drive southeast from Kansas City on Hwy 50 past Warrensburg to the outskirts of Knob Knoster. Turn south on Rte. 132 to the park entrance.

A complete map and directions are available at the Park office. Knob Knoster Park has the 7 mile trail McAdoo Equestrian Trail available to all-terrain cyclists. The Park also features camping, fishing, and picniking.

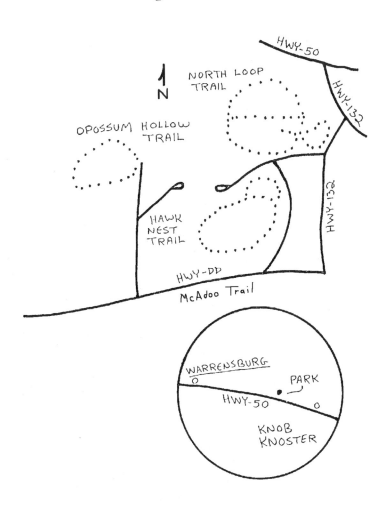

LAWRENCE RIVER FRONT TRAIL

The Lawrence Riverfront Trail is probably the most extensive bicycle trail system in Kansas. More than 50 miles of routes are maintained by the City of Lawrence Parks and Recreation Dept. This trail system is located on top of flood control levees along the Kansas River and on both sides of Clinton Parkway from Iowa Street to Clinton Lake.

Specific information can be obtained through City Hall (913-832-3450) and through both Lawrence bicycle clubs. Contact the Lawrence Bicycling Club, P.O. Box 3596, Lawrence, KS 66046 or Mt. Bike Lawrence, c/o 2708 Lockridge Drive, Lawrence KS 66047.

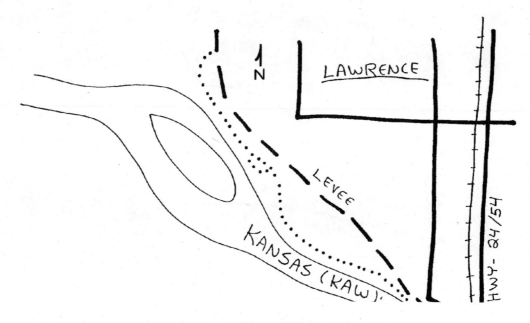

MINOR PARK

T rails of the Blue River (MINOR PARK) are the most popular off road area in Jackson County. The north trail head starts at the parking lot off Red Bridge just east of Holmes Road. The trail continues south to 137th Street.

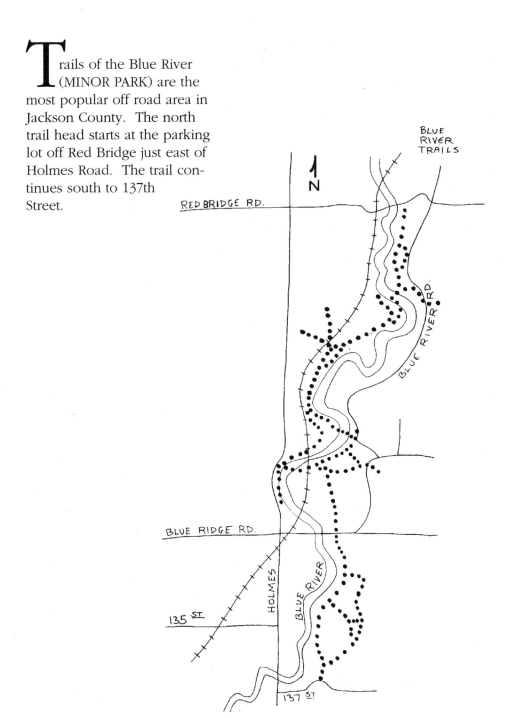

SHAWNEE MISSION PARK

Shawnee Mission Park, located at 79th & Renner Road, has facilities for just about everything but camping. This is the site of the annual Shawnee Mission Triathlon with its very challenging 5+ mile bicycle loop around the lake.

There is a a limited area for offroad just northwest of the lake. Do not use the horse paths for cycling. The Mill Creek Streamway Trail (13 miles) passes the park on the west and may be used for cycling either south or north.

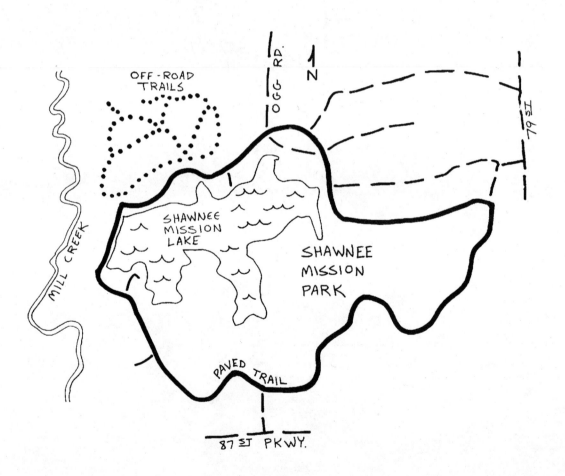

SMITHVILLE LAKE

Smithville Lake, a large man-made lake, is only a short drive north from downtown Kansas City on Hwy 169. The main entrance into Crows Creek Park can easily be reached by driving east on Hwy 92 and then north on Hwy E. There are both paved roads and horse trails around the lake. Check first with the ranger and, as always, please obey the rules of the trail.

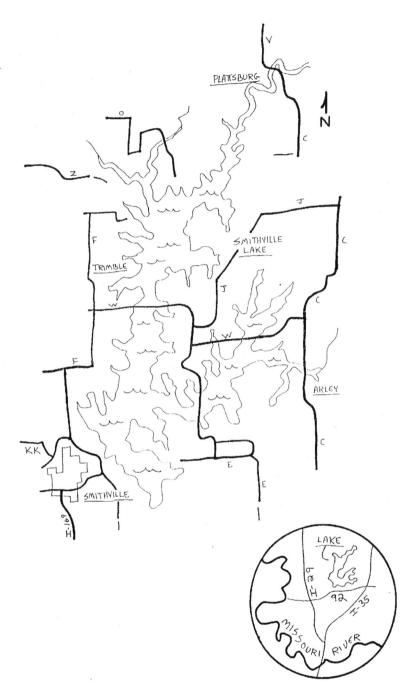

WESTON BEND STATE PARK

Only a 30-40 minute drive north of Kansas City, Weston Bend State Park may be reached from either I-29 or Hwy 45. A three mile paved loop trail winds through the park and is designed to be shared by both hikers and cyclists. There's a parking lot at the trailhead.

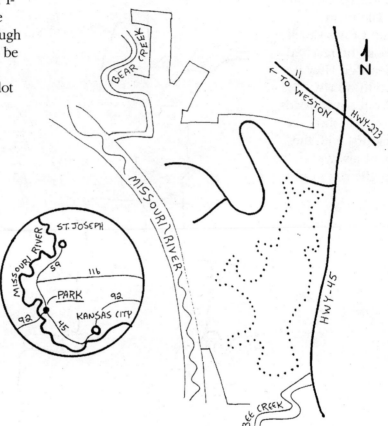

BICYCLE TRAILS

The Kansas City-Lawrence area is blessed with many bike trails and new ones are being added all the time. These existing and projected trails are the result of public/private partnerships in most cases. Several noteworthy ones are The Katy Trail and The Prairie Spirit Trail, both rails-to-trails projects.

Why do they call it a Bike Path? For the most part, these are recreation paths designed for walkers, joggers, on-line skaters, but not cyclists. Bike paths don't enjoy the support of all the cycling community. Because bike paths encourage two way traffic and are generally congested with traffic other than bicycles, a higher incidence of bicycle accidents occur on bike paths versus public roads.

Legislators, most of whom are not cyclists, are of the misguided opinion that the roads are for motor vehicles only. They legislate in favor of bicycle trails with the intention of forcing cyclists into using the trails. Cyclists generally favor a share the road attitude.

What's being done? We are fortunate to have several well conceived bicycle plans for our area thanks to the exhaustive work of Midwest Regional Council (MARC), Johnson-Wyandotte County Parks & Recreation and Lawrence Parks.

Their individual and combined efforts have culminated in studies several times the size of this book. Their plans are public domain for anyone wanting to know the direction and speed of our community becoming "bicycle friendly". Those of us in the "bicycle business" have attended recent public forums and share a cautious optimism.

Page

1. The Prairie Spirit Trail 151

2. The Katy Trail 152

3. Clinton State Park 154

4. Tomahawk–Indian Creek Trails 155

5. Mill Creek Streamway & Shawnee Mission Park 156

6. Longview Lake 157

THE PRAIRIE SPIRIT RAIL-TRAIL

The Prairie Spirit Rail-Trail when completed will stretch for 50 miles from Ottawa in Franklin County through Anderson County to Iola in Allen County. Acquisition of the right-of-way was made possible through "railbanking" under the National Trails System Act. The Department of Wildlife and Parks has a 3 year three phase development plan for this project.

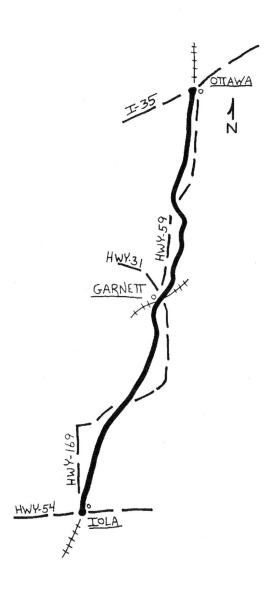

THE KATY TRAIL

THE KATY TRAIL STATE PARK began as a dream of the late investment banker, Edward D. Jones. In September 1986, Governor John Ashcroft directed the Department of Natural Resources to begin development of 200 miles of abandoned KATY rail lines to eventually stretch from Machens northeast of St. Charles westward through Jefferson City to Sedalia.

Since the KATY Trail parallels the Missouri River, much of the area was devastated by the flood of 1993. Currently, all 3 sections are repaired and one can travel eastward from Sedalia to Jefferson City, then to Treloar, and finally to Machens.

For current trail conditions call 1-800-800-KATY

Do I need a mountain bike? No, the trail isn't paved but the surface is firm. The larger tires of the mountain bike make the ride somewhat easier. My most pleasureable ride on the KATY Trail was on a tandem.

Is there bike rental and service available? There are both rental and service at the trail heads. Be prepared with other necessities like spare tubes.

What's there to see? The KATY Trail certainly ranks near the top of Missouri's natural resources. Trains don't run up and down hills, therefore the trail is perfectly flat.

This might be good news for novice cyclists, but it makes for unchallenging riding for the rest of us. Many return froom their first ride on the KATY Trail quite disappointed.

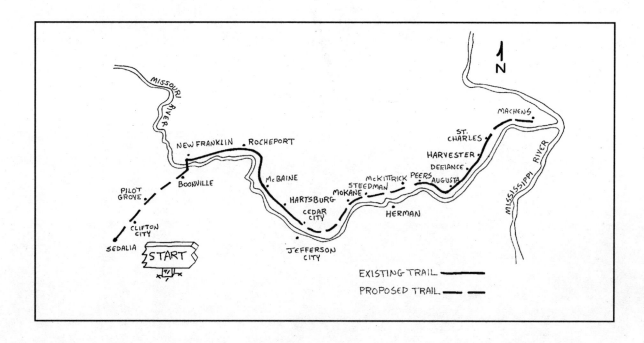

It has to do with expectations. When riding the KATY Trail, take a camera, a picnic lunch, and "stop to smell the flowers." Also, leave the trail at certain points and explore the country side.

Any places to stop for food and drink? Almost every town has a cafe, a tavern, or a general store. Some have Bed & Breakfasts. The School House B & B in Rocheport is a favorite of ours.

The KATY Trail is one of Missouri's finest natural resources. We encourage you to use it but don't abuse it.

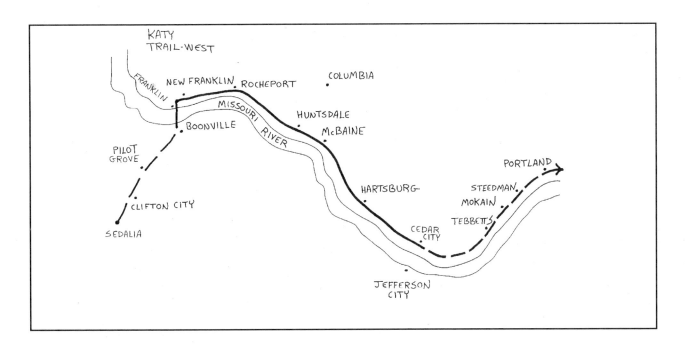

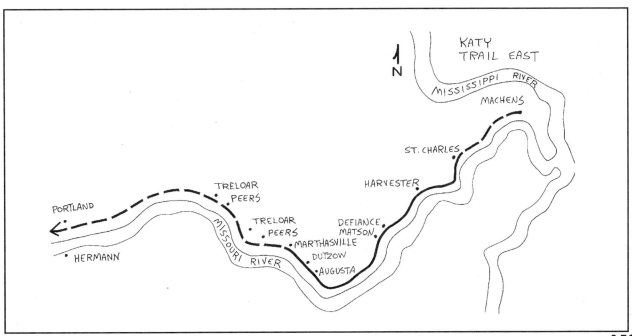

CLINTON STATE PARK

Clinton Lake, southwest of Lawrence, is less than one hour from Kansas City and only a short ride by car or by bicycle from Lawrence west via Clinton Pkwy.

If you're driving from the west, take Hwy 40. For additional information, contact Carl Ringler, Kansas Trails Council coordinator for Clinton Lake at 913-843-9141.

The mountain bike trail at Clinton State Park is considered very competitive. This trail and others are maintained through the efforts of the Kansas Trail Council

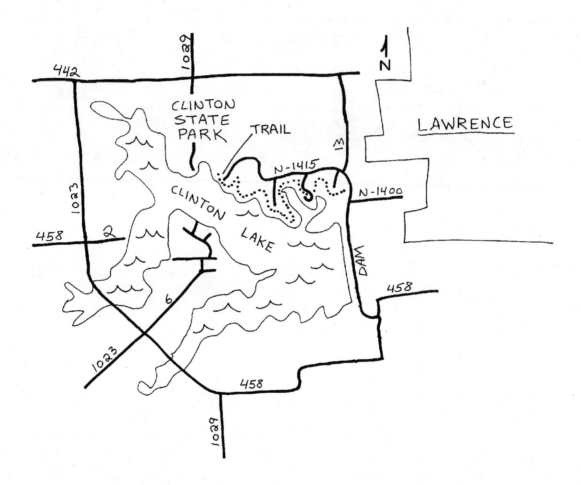

INDIAN CREEK & TOMAHAWK TRAILS

The Indian Creek and Tomahawk Trail system stretches from Cross Creek Park at 119th & Switzer eastward to Hawthorne Valley Park at 124th & Roe. This bike/hike trail extends without interruption through Corporate Woods, Roe Park, Leawood Park, and along the Tomahawk Creek Greenway.

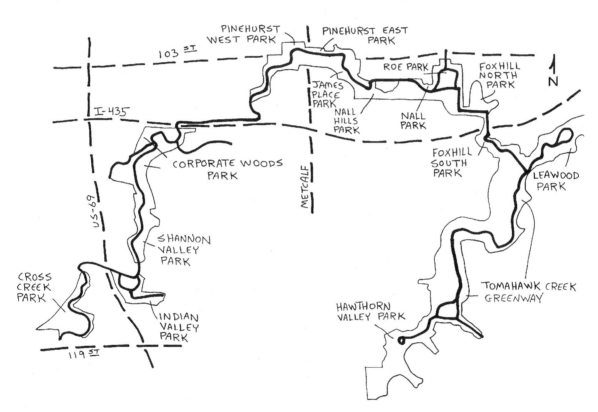

In the next several years, cyclists will be able to travel the Mill Creek Streamway, a 17 mile route, from Olathe area parks north to Shawnee Mission Park and finally to Nelson Island, a 15 acre island in the Kaw River.

Currently, the major portion of this recreation trail travels north from Shawnee Mission Park to Nelson Island, immediately west of I-435 and north of Holliday Drive.

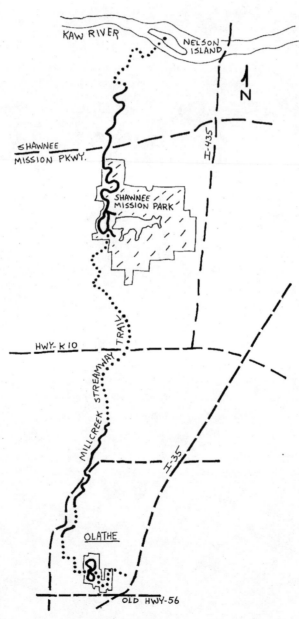

LONGVIEW LAKE

Starting Point: Parking lot, start of bike trail, south on Raytown Rd.

Distance: 12-14 (each lap)

Degree of Difficulty: N/A

Terrain: excellent for cycling

Things To See: Excellent area for all kinds of cycling; historic Long Farm; new home subdivisions; Longview Community College; convenience store on Highgrove.

Take I-470 to Raytown Road, head south on Raytown Rd. to parking lot. Cycle north on Raytown Road across Highgrove Rd north with lake on your right. RIGHT at 109th across dam RIGHT on View High Rd, past golf course, past 3rd St., and past entrance to Long Farm

RIGHT on Sampson thru housing area
RIGHT at Scherer Road, up and then down big hills to starting point.
This ride may be done counter clockwise.

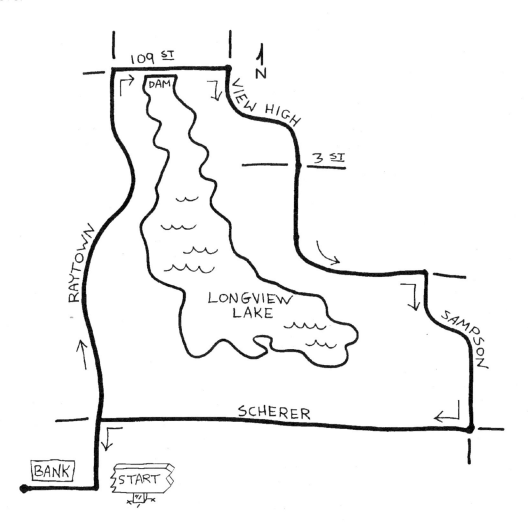

HOW TO BUY A BIKE

Writing an article on How To Buy A Bike is an interesting challenge. When this question is posed to five veteran cyclists, you're bound to get five different answers. It's about as controversial a question as which computer to purchase, IBM,

---

My first commandment of buying a bicycle:
THOU SHALT NOT BUY A BICYCLE AT A STORE THAT SELLS MICROWAVES

Macintosh, or a PC.

In other words, seek out the expert advice of someone in a store that specializes in bicycles. Find someone who will ask you the right questions, listen to your answers, and then patiently fit you with the appropriate size and model.

Remember, if you've reached your full growth (not girth), most bicycles can and will last a decade. Therefore, it's important that the bicycle fit you both physically and according to your needs. The store where you buy your bicycle is the most likely place where you'll return to have it serviced. Your bicycle dealer depends upon your satisfaction, not only to return for service and accessories, but also to recommend him to others.

This article is not intended to sound as though we're preaching. We suggest you read the following pages listing area bicycle dealers, and select someone convenient for you. Then, follow the steps below keeping in mind that the best service is usually not during the busiest store hours. A trip to get your bike repaired is not quite like passing through the drive-up window at McDonalds.

It is not unusual today for an experienced cyclist to own both a road bike and a mountain bike. Once you've finalized that difficult decision of what bike to buy, you still need the following accessories:
✔ approved helmet
✔ water bottle & cage for the bottle
✔ pump to carry on the bike
✔ spare tube
✔ bike tool kit
✔ saddle pouch
✔ comfortable saddle

And, finally, several tips:
✔ ride with a partner in the beginning
✔ try an organized ride
✔ don't fill your bike tires at the filling station
✔ take a maintenance course at the bike shop or through a club

Buying a good bicycle is the most important decision you can make right now. The rest of the information in this Guide is meaningless without owning a good bicycle.

Here are 3 mandatory steps to follow in shopping for a bicycle:

Determine the kind of riding you'll be doing and discuss is candidly with the bike dealer. If you're a newcomer, your skills will improve dramatically. Typically, less experienced buyers refer to Consumer Report or some bicycle magazine for their information.

Test ride several models and always wear a helmet. Remember, you're riding a strange vehicle.

Price and style are two important components of your final decision. If you choose to buy a $100.00 bicycle from the discount store, you'll wind up doing most of the work. As you step up in price, the higher priced bicycle is made of lighter and more efficient components which tend to make riding easier and more enjoyable. Consider that for each $100.00 spent on a bicycle, it's only $8.33 each month for a year. You owe yourself that extra quality.Bicycle styles fall into three general categories: sport-touring, mountain-off road, and cross terrain (hybrid).

BIKE DEALERS

JOHNSON COUNTY DEALERS
BIKESOURCE	119th & Quivira, Overland Park, KS	451-1515
Bike America	9514 Nall, Overland Park KS	381-5431
Bike America	417 N. Rawhide Drive, Olathe KS	780-4500
Bikes For The Likes Of Us	9052 E. 50 Hwy, Raytown MO	356-7070
The Bike Rack	7945 Santa Fe, Overland Park, KS	642-6115
Turners Cycling & Fitness	8909 Santa Fe, Overland Park KS	381-5298
Tri Tech Sports	12948 W. 87th, Lenexa, KS	363-2443
Wheeler's Cycle & Fitness	12205 West 63rd, Shawnee KS	268-1122
Leawood Bicycle & Athletic Gear	12311 State Line, Kansas City MO	942-4442

LAWRENCE DEALERS
Cycle Works	1601 W. 23rd, Lawrence, KS	(913) 842-6363
Rick's Bike Shop	916 Massachusetts, Lawrence KS	(913) 841-6642
Bike America	2223 Louisiana, Lawrence, KS	(913) 842-8744
The Sunflower Group	804 Massachusetts, Lawrence KS	(913) 843-5000

NORTHLAND
River Market Cyclery	312 Delaware, Kansas City MO	842-2453
Mike's Bicycle Adventure	6222 N. Chatham Ave, Kansas City MO	741-2400
Biscari Bros. Bicycles	884 S. 291, Liberty MO	792-8877
Bike Works Cycling & Fitness	6565 N. Oak Tfwy, Gladstone MO	436-5636
The Wheel	5126 N. Antioch, Kansas City MO	455-2453
Sunshine Bicycles	352 S. 291 Hwy, Liberty MO	231-133

JACKSON COUNTY DEALERS
Bike Stop	4201 S. Noland Rd, Independence, MO	478-1175
BIKESOURCE	231 SE Main, Lee's Summit MO	525-6000
Pace Bicycle Haven	1215 W. Lexington, Independence MO	461-7433
Peddler's	139 E. Lexington, Independence MO	254-6855
Peddler's	325 E. 3rd Street, Lee's Summit MO	524-1819
Peddler's	1318 N. 7th, Blue Springs MO	229-6262
BIKESOURCE	4118 Pennsylvania, Kansas City MO	736-3400
Midwest Cyclery	3957 Broadway, Kansas City MO	931-4653
Wheelers Cycle & Fitness	8345 Wornall, Kansas City MO	363-2443
Waldo Bike Shop	507 W. 75th, Kansas City MO	333-6595
The Bike Shack	10414 Blue Ridge Blvd, Kansas City MO	761-3233
Biscari Bros. Bicycles	5116 Independence Ave, Kansas City MO	231-1331

Organized cycling should not be thought of as the opposite of disorganized cycling. When you read the biographical sketches of the contributors to this book, each found his or her way into cycling through a club or an organization.

If it weren't for organized cycling, I would never have been compelled to write cycling guide books.Several months into cycling, I joined up with a Saturday morning group of about 30 cyclists. A self-proclaimed leader distributed maps and then led us on a 30-40 mile journey with a pleasant stop en route for breakfast.

There was neither a charge for the service nor a requirement to join the organization.

Almost every new cyclist suffers through several trips around the neighborhood or the school or church parking lot, before venturing forth "on the road."

It's similar to learning to drive a car, although some seem never to master that skill. As a word of caution, avoid those mutipurpose bike and recreation trails during your first several weeks of cycling. They're too narrow for oncoming bikes to pass and they're too congested with other traffic. But, this caveat does not apply to The KATY Trail.

Bicycle clubs and organizations are the life blood of cycling. Whtever your interest or skill level, there's an organization or club for you. Their modest membership fees will enable you to make new bicycling friends and to receive a newsletter filled with cycling tours and other related cycling activities.

The following is an alphabetical listing of area bicycle clubs.

1. *Earth Riders*
2. *Eastern JacksonCounty Wheelmen*
3. *Easy Riders Bicycle Club*
4. *Johnson County Bicycle Club*
5. *Kansas City Bicycle Club*
6. *Northbland (KCBC) Bicycle Club*
7. *Leavenworth Bicycle Club*

EARTH RIDERS is a newcomer to the Kansas City cycling and already boasts a membership of more than 80. This group is dedicated to off road cycling. They meet monthly on a Wedneday evening at Torre's Pizza in The City Market. For further information contact either Wade Frerichs (531-7302) or Mike Hamilton (741-2400)

JOHNSON COUNTY BIKE CLUB (JCBC) is organized for the purpose of promotion of safe and recreational bicycling for all ages and abilities. Meetings are held on the first Tuesday of the month. The JCBC can be reached by mail at Box 2203, Shawnee Mission, KS 66201 or by calling 649-2900 (Hotline).

EASY RIDERS is a very loosely organized group of men and women bicyclists who have retired or wish they could. They try to ride regularly. Rides are scheduled for Tuesdays, Thursdays, and Saturdays on the Indian Creek Bike/Hike Trail in Leawood and Overland Park. Rides usually start at Leawood Park (119th and Tomahawk Creek Parkway). No great effort is made to make the rides in the shortest possible time. The pace is determined by the slowest rider. A few rest stops are scheduled to allow time for conversation and sharing of jokes and stories. If the Easy Riders appeals to you, contact Jim Burruss (523-2549) or Don Inbody (642-5431)

EASTERN JACKSON COUNTY WHEELMEN meets at The Bike Stop the first Tuesday at 7:30 PM in season. Contact Todd Pennington (478-1175) of The Bike Stop.

ORGANIZED CYCLING

KANSAS CITY BICYCLE CLUB (KCBC) is the oldest and the largest in the area. The meeting are the first Friday of each month at 7:30 PM at St. Paul's Episcopal Church, 40th & Main. The Club is affiliated with League of American Bicyclists and the USCF. KCBC publishes a monthly newsletter with current ride schedules. For membership information, mail to P.O. Box 412163, Kansas City, MO 64141 or call Tim Osburn (816) 781-8028.

NORTHLAND KCBC is a very active organization that leads interesting rides evenings during the week and weekends. For addiitional information contact David Van Wyck at (816) 741-7559.

LAWRENCE BICYCLE CLUB, P.O. Box 3596, Lawrence, KS 66046 has sponsored the "Classic Octoginta" every October for the past 26 years. This club embodies the spirit and the mission of bicycle clubs. Contact Jim Turner (913-842-5174), Jim Baze (913-842-6073), Tim Timmons (913-843-2722), or Mike Bryan (913-842-8299)

LEAVENWORTH BICYCLE CLUB is a very active organization with monthly meetings. The club sponsors rides evening during the week and on the weekend. Many of the rides in this Guide are from Joel Buck(913-682-7449) and Greg Scircle (913-682-8918). They welcome your calls about cycling in the Leavenworth area.

The following is a partial list of names and addresses of national organizations which serve the specialized needs of bicyclists.

Bicycle Federation of America
1818 R St., NW, Washington, DC 20009
Promotes all aspects of cycling, publishes Pro Bike News, conducts research on safety and bike-trail planning.

Adventure Cycling c/o Bikecentennial.
P.O.Box 8398, Missoula, MT 59807
National non-profit group promotes touring, leads extended bike tours. An annual membership fee of $22.00 entitles one to 9 issues of BikeReport magazine, more than 19,000 miles of bicycle routes through Cyclosource catalog, the Cyclists' Yellow Pages reference book, and a wide selection of on- and off-road tours.A great source of transcontinental bicycle maps.

International Randonneurs
727 N. Salina St., Syracuse, NY 13224
Organization for long-distance cycling; sponsors U.S. qualifying rides for Paris-Brest-Paris event.

League of American Bicyclists
Suite 209, 6707 Whitestone Rd., Baltimore, MD 21207. The oldest U.S. cycling organization and a major advocacy group. Membership open to everyone.

National Off-Road Bicycle Association (NORBA) serves as the national governing organization for mountain biking. An annual membership fee of $25.00 affords members eligibility for all NORBA races, an off-road competition guide, 12 monthly issues of NORBA News, insurance at NORBA races, and an opportunity to participate in mountain bike clinics. NORBA, One Olympic Plaza, Colorado Springs, CO 80909   (719) 578-4717

Rails to Trails Conservancy
1400 16th St., NW, Washington, DC 20036
National organization that promotes conversion of disuse railroad beds to hiking/biking trails. The KATY Trail is a part of this program.

The Tandem Club of America
c/o Jack Goetz, 2220 Vaness Dr., Birmingham, AL 35242 Sponsors events, publishes a newsletter

U.S. Cycling Federation
1750 E. Boulder St., Colorado Springs, CO 80909. Oversees amateur bicycle racing and Olympic training.

BICYCLE ADVOCACY

The simplest explanation of bicycle advocacy is making your community more "bicycle friendly." Both novice and veteran cyclists quickly appreciate the challenges of sharing the road with other vehicles.

Bicycle advocacy is nothing new. The League of American Bicyclists (LAB), the nation's oldest bicycle advocacy group, was founded in the 1880's. The LAW, as it was called until recently, established its Good Roads Campaign to improve roads for all users. In 1890, the League boasted nearly 100,000 members.

The L.A.W. Good Roads Campaign was so successful that it helped to increase the popularity of the automobile which subsequently brought about the decline of the bicycle as a means of transportation.

Today, we're witnessing what some call the second "golden age" of bicycling. Unfortuntely, neither road construction nor transportation legislation have kept pace with the increase in bicycle usage. The Federal Transportation Act of 1991 is the first serious legislation enacted to address the problems of bicyclists and pedestrians.

The Intermodal Surface Transportation Effeciency Act (ISTEA) has mandated that each state name a bicycle-pedestrian coordinator.

Missouri coordinator is Dennis Scott. Dennis operates within the jurisdiction of the Missouri Highway and Transportation Department and can be reached as follows:
Dennis Scott, Missouri Bicycle-Pedestrian Coordinator Missouri Highway and Transportation Department Jefferson City, MO 65102

Kansas coordinator is Marc Bechtel. Mark operates under KDOT and can be reached as follows:
Mark Bechtel
Kansas Department of Transportation
217 SE 4th
Topeka, KS 66603
(913) 296-7448

Local and state advocacy contacts include:

Kansas Bicycle Alliance (KANBIKE)
P.O. Box 2031
Shawnee Mission, KS 66201
(913-967-7100)
This relatively new organiztion has already made its presence felt in legislative circles. It's our only cycling Voice in Kansas. Please support KANBIKE.

Missouri Bicycle Federation
P.O. Box 104871,
Jefferson City, MO 65110 (314-636-4488)

A nonprofit cycling advocacy group founded in March of 1993. The group has statewide representation that speaks as a united body for or against issues affecting cyclists. MBF's mission is to make Missouri a better place to ride through the advancement of bicycle access, safety, and education. Any cyclist who shares similar thoughts should contact the Missouri Bicycle Federation at (314) 636-4488. The newsletter, The HUB, is very informative

These advocacy organizations depend upon your input and your support. There are more opportunities for cyclists to improve their position in the transportation world today than ever before.

If you are interested in other bicycle and pedestrian issues at a national level, contact one of the following.

Don't complain about the plight of cyclists. There are so many advocacy groups available today at the local, state, and national level. Stand up and be counted. Make your voice heard.

The League of American Bicyclists (LAB)
190 W. Ostend St., Suite 120
Baltimore, MD 21230
(410) 539-3399
Specializes in rallies, bicycle club activities and advocacy at the national and local level.

Adventure Cycling
c/o Bikecentennial
P.O. Box 8308
Missoula, MT 59807
(406) 721-1776
Specializes in bicycle touring, mapping, long distance bicycle routes and advocacy.

Rails-to-Trails Conservancy
1400 16th St. NW, Suite 300
Washington, DC 20036
(202) 797-5400
Promotes the conversion of abandoned railroad corridors to multi-use trails.

Bicycle Federation of America
1818 E St. NW, Washington, DC 20009
Promotes walking and bicycling as efficient and environmentally friendly transportation modes. The National Bicycle and Pedestrian Advocacy Campaign is a BFA project supported by grants from several foundations.

OVERNITE TRIPS

One of the many joys of cycling is an overnight bicycle trip with either camping or a stay at a Bed & Breakfast. The following list is in no way all inclusive. Most of these we've either tried personally or heard about from a reliable source.

ROCHEPORT Drive to either Rocheport off I-70 just west of Columbia or to Jefferson City. Stay at The School House B & B, 3rd & Clark Street, Rocheport, MO 65279 (314-698-2022). Advance reservations are definitely needed. If you plan to cycle from Jefferson City to Rocheport, as I have, drop your overnight stuff at the B & B on the way.

FULTON Wonderful cycling around historic Westminster college and the country side. Stay at Loganberry Inn, 310 W. 7th, Fulton, MO 65251 (314-642-9229) Four unique guest rooms. Located 7 miles south of I-70 on U.S. 5

JAMESPORT This is Amish country located about 70 miles northeast of Kansas City on Mo 6 after exiting I-35 at Gallatin. Places to stay include the Richardson House B & B, Jamesport, MO (816-684-6664) with only two guestroom and you rent the complete house. A short distance further east is The Hyde Mansion B & B, 418 E 7th, Trenton ((816-359-5631) This was the dream home of Missouri governor Arthur M. Hyde. It has six guest rooms and is very comfortable.

The Jamesport area has excellent cycling. Often times you share the road with a horse-drawn buggy. Cycling from one Amish country store to another makes for a memorable day.

For you campers, Crowder State Park, offers a swimming lake with a sand beach, and a secluded camp site. Plan to get your campsite early on 'in season' weekends.

LIBERTY & EXCELSIOR SPRINGS Try Lindgren's Landing B & B, 222 West Franklin in Liberty (816-781-8742) or Crescent Lake Manor, 1261 St. Louis St. in Excelsior Springs (816-637-2958). Both areas are good for cycling. Refer to some of the routes in this book.

WESTON Stay at either Apple Creek B & B, 908 Washington, Weston (816-386-5724) or Benner House B & B, 645 Main St (816-386-2616) Cycling is hilly but good around Weston. Travel south to Platte City, or west to Atchison and Leavenworth.

PARKKVILLE Stay at either Down To Earth Lifestyles, Rte 22, Parkville (816-891-1018) or Parkville House B & B, 504 Main St, Parkville (816-587-0463). The English Landing in Parkville is a great place to start a ride, many of which are featured in this book.

VALLEY FALLS The Barn B & B is featured in the Leavenworth section.

COUNCIL GROVE The Cottage House Hotel, 25 North Neosho, Council Grove, KS 66846 (316-767-6828) of Flint Hills B & B, 613 W. Main, Council Grove, KS 66846

are both excellent choices. This area is of historic significance for the Santa Fe Trail and other points of interest.

Council Grove can be reached by travelling I-70 west to Topeka and either taking I-70 or I-35 and looking for turnoffs to Council Grove.

There are a wide selection of cycling routes. For campers, we recommend staying at Council Grove Lake and cycling from there. A trip south to Strong City will take you to Z-Bar Ranch and the Flint Hills.

LAWRENCE has excellent camping facilities at Clinton and Lone Star Lakes. Both areas are featured in the Lawrence section of this book.

HILLSDALE LAKE provides an excellent combination of off road and paved road cycling plus camping facilities.

KANSAS CITY features an endless list of interesting Bed & Breakfasts.

Southmoreland On The Plaza, 116 E. 46th, Kansas City, MO 64112 (816-531-7979) This 12-room Colonia Revival 1913 mansion is walking distance from The Plaza. It's recommended for all cyclists except those on a tight budget.

We aren't in the business of rating B & B's. The above are ones we've tried or have had recommended by friends. Our apologies to the many fine establishments that we failed to mention.

BICYCLE CALENDAR

SUNDAY

✔ The Colonel's Ride, 2:00 PM, Loose Park

✔ KCBC Training Race, 8:30 AM, Leawood Bicycles

✔ Leavenworth Bike Club Sunrise Rides, 303 N 5th, 7:00 AM

✔ Bill's Burrito Blast, 2nd Sunday, JCCC, 10:00 AM

✔ Northland KCBC, Hardee's Metro North, 1:30 PM

✔ KCBC Independence SNG, MCI, 1:30 PM

MONDAY

✔ Normandy Courts Club House, 97th & North Oak, 6:00 PM

✔ Skip Work & Ride, Venture 63rd & Pflumm, 8:00 AM

TUESDAY

✔ 75th Street Brewery Ride, 6:30 PM, 75th St Brewery

✔ Northland KCBC Show-N-Go, 6:30 PM, Hy-Vee Grocery, 72nd & N. Prospect

✔ JCBC Shawnee Mission Park Marina, 6:30 PM

✔ KCBC Mason Elem School, Lee's Summit, 5:00 PM

✔ Jackson County Wheelmen, Lakewood QuikTrip, 6:00 PM

✔ Prairie Village SNG, Waids Restaurant, 8:00 AM

✔ Easy Riders, Roe Park, Roe just south of 103rd, 9:20 AM

WEDNESDAY

✔ KCBC Beginners Ride, 6:30 PM, 18th & Fayette, NKC

✔ Mike, The Plumber's Friend Ride, 6:30 PM, 83rd & Wornall

✔ Leavenworth Bike Club, Bud's Warehouse 20th & Spruce, 5:45 PM

THURSDAY

✔ Northland Show-N-Go, 6:00 PM, Boardwalk S.C.

✔ Westport Brewing Company Ride, 6:00 PM, Muldoon's in Westport

✔ Lakewood Show-N-Go, 6:00 PM, Lakewood QuikTrip

✔ KCBC Race Team Training Race, call 942-4442

✔ JCBC Ride, 6:00 PM, Shawnee Mission West HS

✔ Jackson County Wheelmen, Bike Stop Independence, 6:00 PM

✔ KCBC SNG, MCI Hospital, 6:00 PM

✔ JCBC SNG, SM West HS, 6:00 PM

✔ JCBC, Laird Park on Johnson Drive, Shawnee, 6:15 PM

✔ KCBC Racers Training Ride, 143rd & Kenneth, 6:30 PM

✔ Easy Riders, Corporate Woods, 10:00 AM

FRIDAY

SATURDAY

✔ KCBC Training Ride, 8:30 AM, Leawood Bicycles

✔ Northland Show-N-Go, 10:00 AM, KC North Community Center

✔ KCBC Show-N-Go, 8:00 AM, Waid's in Prairie Village

✔ Leavenworth Bike Club Fitness Rides from Leeavenworth Park, 8:00 AM

✔ Jackson County Wheelmen SNG, Lakewood QuikTrip, 8:00 AM

✔ JCBC Dirt Ride, Minor Park, Red Bridge Rd, 9:00 AM

✔ JCBC SNG, Tri Tech Sports, 8:30 AM

✔ Easy Riders, Leawood Park, 119th & Roe, 9:00 AM

BIBLIOGRAPHY

The following is a partial list of books available on cycling. They are in random order and available only at full line book stores, some bicycle stores, and major libraries. On several of the major titles, we have included addresses. A (✔) mark indicates books we've particularly enjoyed.

Bikecentennial, P.O. Box 8308, Missoula, MT 59807. A complete directory to everything related to cycling. (✔)

The Bicyclist's SourceBook by Leccese and Plevin, $16.95, Woodbine House, 5615 Fishers Lane, Rockville, MD 20852. As complete a bicycle reference book as we've found. (✔)

Effective Cycling by John Forester, $17.95, MIT Press, 55 Hayward St., Cambridge, MA 02142. Considered by most to be the bible of cycling. Available also in videotape. (✔)

The Bicycle Repair Book by Rob Van der Plas

The Bicycle Touring Manual by Rob Van der Plas, $16.95

Training For Cycling by Davis Phinney and Connie Carpenter

Anybody's Bike Book by Tom Cuthbertson, $9.95, An original manual of bicycle repairs.

Bike Touring, The Sierra Club Guide to Outings on Wheels, $10.95

Bicycle Magazine Cycling Series, Rodale Press, 33 E. Minor St., Emmaus, PA 18098
- Cycling For Women
- Bicycle Repair
- Bicycle Touring
- Easy Bicycle Maintenance
- Fitness Through Cycling
- Mountain Bikes
- Ride Like A Pro
- Riding and Racing Techniques
- Training For Endurance

Bicycle Magazine's Complete Guide, $16.95 (✔)

Glenn's New Complete Bicycle Manual by Clarence Coles and Harold Green, $23.00

Richards' Ultimate Bicycle Book by Richard Ballantine and Richard Grant, $29.95 (✔)

Fat Tire Rider, Everyone's Guide to Mountain Biking by Kennedy, Kloser, & Samer $19.95

Complete Book of Bicycling by Greg LeMond, $11.00

Cycling - A Celebration of the Sport and the World's Best Places to Enjoy It by Arlene Plevin, $12.00

The Complete Book of Bicycling by Eugene A Sloan, $15.95

Mountain Bike! by William Nealy $12.95

HIKING Kansas City by Willam Eddy & Ricahrd Ballantine, $6.95

Magazines:
BICYCLING, 33 E. Minor Street, Emmaus, PA 18049
BICYCLE GUIDE, 711 Boylston STreet, Boston, MA 02116

Racing Magazines:
VELONEWS, 5595 Arapahoe Ave., Suite G, Boulder, CO 80303
WINNING, 1127 Hamilton St., Allentown, PA 18102

CAST OF CHARACTERS

STEVE KATZ-AUTHOR

RON BERRY-PHOTOGRAPHER

RANDY SEBA-GRAPHIC DESIGN & LAYOUT

MIKE OGDEN - MAPMAKER

BOB BLISS - CARTOONIST